Microsoft®

PowerPoint® 2010 Plain & Simple

Nancy Muir

Published with the authorization of Microsoft Corporation by:
O'Reilly Media, Inc.
1005 Gravenstein Highway North
Sebastopol, California 95472

Printed and bound in the United States of America.

3 4 5 6 7 8 9 10 11 QG 7 6 5 4 3 2

Microsoft Press titles may be purchased for educational, business or sales promotional use. Online editions are also available for most titles (*http://my.safaribooksonline.com*). For more information, contact our corporate/institutional sales department: (800) 998-9938 or *corporate@ oreilly.com*. Visit our website at *microsoftpress.oreilly.com*. Send comments to *mspinput@microsoft.com*.

Microsoft, Microsoft Press, ActiveX, Excel, FrontPage, Internet Explorer, PowerPoint, SharePoint, Webdings, Windows, and Windows 7 are either registered trademarks or trademarks of Microsoft Corporation in the United States and/or other countries. Other product and company names mentioned herein may be the trademarks of their respective owners.

Unless otherwise noted, the example companies, organizations, products, domain names, e-mail addresses, logos, people, places, and events depicted herein are fictitious, and no association with any real company, organization, product, domain name, e-mail address, logo, person, place, or event is intended or should be inferred.

This book expresses the author's views and opinions. The information contained in this book is provided without any express, statutory, or implied warranties. Neither the author, O'Reilly Media, Inc., Microsoft Corporation, nor their respective resellers or distributors, will be held liable for any damages caused or alleged to be caused either directly or indirectly by such information.

Acquisitions and Developmental Editor: Kenyon Brown
Production Editor: Rachel Monaghan
Editorial Production: Online Training Solutions, Inc.
Technical Reviewer: George Cain, Box Twelve Communications, Inc.
Indexer: Potomac Indexing, LLC
Compositor: Ron Bilodeau
Illustrator: Robert Romano

978-0-735-62728-4

[2012-04-13]

To Ebb

Contents

11 Formatting Text, Objects, and Slides 143

12 Adding Transitions and Animations 167

13 Finalizing Your Slide Show 179

What do you think of this book? We want to hear from you!

Microsoft is interested in hearing your feedback so we can continually improve our books and learning resources for you. To participate in a brief online survey, please visit:

www.microsoft.com/learning/booksurvey/

Acknowledgments

Thanks to Ken Brown of O'Reilly Media for leading the charge on this title, and to Juliana Aldous of Microsoft Press for signing me up to work on the book originally. Also, my gratitude to Rachel Monaghan at O'Reilly for coordinating various production aspects of the book, and to George Cain for his able technical editing and John Pierce for the great job copy editing the book.

1

About This Book

If you are the typical PowerPoint user, you lead a hectic life, whether you spend time running from meeting to meeting and conference to conference or from the soccer match to a volunteer committee meeting. If so, this book is for you. In *Microsoft PowerPoint 2010 Plain & Simple*, you get an easy-to-use reference that helps you get to work immediately. My goals are to help you start building presentations right away and to provide you with information about all sorts of tools and features you can use to create more sophisticated presentations over time.

This book is based on Microsoft PowerPoint 2010 installed on the Windows 7 operating system, but if you have an earlier version of Windows (preferably Windows XP or Windows Vista with available service packs installed), you'll find that most things work just the same. The great new features that PowerPoint 2010 introduces make your work easier to handle and offer some powerful visual tools for your presentations.

No Computerese!

With a presentation deadline staring you in the face, the last thing you want is a lengthy lecture. You need to find out how to accomplish something quickly. This book is structured task by task to help you find what you need help with now and to keep you moving.

No task in this book makes you read more than two pages to find an answer to your question. Look up what you need to do in the table of contents or index, follow the steps in the task, and you're done. I don't spend lots of time on elaborate explanations, and you don't need a technical dictionary by your side to understand the steps I describe.

Occasionally, you encounter a See Also element that refers you to a related task simply because some functions overlap each other. You can also find tips here and there that provide advice. Finally, the Try This feature gives you ideas for how to put PowerPoint to use, and Caution elements warn you of potential problems. But the main focus of this book is to keep you on track, providing the information you need quickly and simply.

Just Essential Tasks

The tasks in this book are organized logically for the types of things you do in PowerPoint 2010. If you've never built a presentation, you can start at the beginning and work your way through to create your first slide show. But you don't have to move through the book in order. If you know exactly what you want to accomplish, just find that task and go to it!

And the Easiest Way to Do Them

Although PowerPoint 2010 often gives you several ways to get things done, I've tried to suggest the easiest way to get results. The PowerPoint user interface (what you see on the screen) introduced in PowerPoint 2007 and carried on in PowerPoint 2010 has gotten rid of some methods you might be used to, such as using menus and toolbars for most tasks, but keyboard shortcuts and contextual toolbars (tools that appear when you perform a certain type of task) are still available to address different styles of working. I encourage you to explore the user interface and Help system to find other ways of getting things done after you master the basics.

A Quick Overview

Although you don't have to read this book from front to back (in fact, you probably won't), it's useful to understand how I've structured it so that you can find your way around.

After you install PowerPoint 2010 (an easy task because the Microsoft Office installer guides you through step by step), you can begin exploring any of the following sections and their individual tasks.

Sections 2 and 3 introduce you to what's new in PowerPoint 2010 and the PowerPoint user interface and explain how you move around and work with tools and views in the program.

Sections 4, 5, 6, and 7 start you out building the text portion of a presentation by adding text to individual slides in a graphical environment, by using slide masters (tools that allow you to quickly and easily make changes to global design and text settings that apply to all your slides, handouts, or notes pages), and by entering information into a familiar outline format. You also learn essential information such as how to open and save a presentation and how to get help. You become acquainted with placeholders on slides, which can contain either text or objects, and begin to understand how you build a presentation slide by slide and view the results.

Sections 8, 9, 10, and 11 are where you begin to look at the overall look and feel of slides in various views. You also work with the design aspect of your presentation, using various layouts (different combinations of placeholders and content) and themes that contain color and graphical elements. You work with inserting and handling various objects, such as clip art, WordArt, videos, and pictures. These sections also provide valuable information on how to format text and other objects in your presentation so that it looks polished and professional.

Sections 12 and 13 take you near to your goal of a final presentation by providing information about slick animations and transitions that you can add to your slides to bring them to life. You also learn about how to set up your show to run as you want it to and how to rehearse, proof, and generally ensure that your presentation is letter perfect.

Sections 14, 15, and 16 help you actually give your presentation to others, either by running it in person, printing out hard copies of it, sharing it via e-mail, or publishing it to the Web. This is what all the rest of the work is for, and if you do your job right, you can provide a well-written and well-designed presentation to your audience.

Finally, Section 17 offers information about a few more advanced tools in PowerPoint 2010 that you might want to explore after you master the basics. Among other things, you discover how to work with presentation templates to save you time, create custom shows from your larger presentation, customize tools on the ribbon tabs, and even work with PowerPoint presentations from your cell phone.

A Few Assumptions

When you write a book, you have to first think about your readers. Who are they, what do they already know, and what do they need to know? In writing this book, I've assumed that you are essentially computer literate—you know how to turn your computer on and off, what a mouse is and how to click and double-click items with it, and how to select text or objects. I also assume that you have worked with some kind of software and have at least a passing acquaintance with tool buttons, dialog boxes, and software menus made up of various commands.

Whether you use your computer every day in a high-powered job or spend most of your computer time playing games and writing notes to friends, I assume you have an Internet connection and have been on the Internet. Other than that, this book tries to provide all the steps you need to accomplish the tasks within it in a straightforward way—with plenty of graphics to help you see what I'm talking about.

What's New in PowerPoint 2010?

If you worked with PowerPoint 2007, you already know about the ribbon, a set of tools that you access on tabs. One major change to that interface in PowerPoint 2010 is the addition of the Office Backstage view, which contains commands and options that you used to work with through the Office button but that you now access through the File tab.

If you only used Office programs prior to Office 2007, you need to become familiar with the ribbon. These tools occasionally offer galleries of choices, and when you move your mouse over these choices, they are previewed on your slides before you apply them. Sometimes when you work on certain functions, specialized tabs appear; for example, if you select a drawing object, the Drawing Tools, Format tab appears.

PowerPoint 2010 offers improvements to visual elements, including better picture and video formatting tools, and additional themes and SmartArt choices.

Finally, PowerPoint 2010 offers more features for sharing presentations with others and broadcasting slide shows on the Internet. I think you'll like what you see once you absorb the changes. PowerPoint 2010 is all about making the tools you work with accessible and obvious.

The Final Word

This book is designed to make your learning painless, with plenty of visual information to help you pick things up at a glance, along with easy-to-follow steps. My goals are to give you what you need, make tasks easy to find and understand, and help you have fun learning to work with PowerPoint 2010, which is a great design tool that helps you communicate more effectively.

I hope you find the tasks in this book helpful and that you are producing award-winning presentations in no time.

What's New in PowerPoint 2010?

If you are making the move from Microsoft Office PowerPoint 2003 to PowerPoint 2010, you'll find that it sports an interface that offers a somewhat different way of getting things done. After investing a little time getting used to the new tools and features, you'll find that this version of PowerPoint is actually easier to use, although you have a small learning curve to go through. If you worked with PowerPoint 2007, you've got a head start on this new look and approach to getting things done.

This section is where you get your first look at PowerPoint 2010, discovering where various tools and settings reside and learning how to use the newest features, such as the File tab and Office Backstage.

Other than the selections offered through the File tab, which provides file-management commands such as New, Open, Save, and Print, most features are available as buttons on tabs on the ribbon. In some cases, panes are displayed, such as the Research or the Clip Art pane.

Galleries of graphical selections allow you to preview how effects look on your slides or objects before you apply them, and several enhanced galleries and formatting options are available to explore in PowerPoint 2010. Finally, in this section I introduce you to new features, such as sections, Animation Painter, and broadcasting slide shows.

What's Where in PowerPoint 2010?

PowerPoint 2010 uses a central ribbon of tools that you access on various tabs. The tools on the tabs are broken into groups. In addition, the Quick Access Toolbar lets you place your favorite tools in one location and access functions that aren't offered through the ribbon. Some tools on the ribbon display drop-down galleries of selections, and others open dialog boxes for making detailed settings.

You access the File menu by clicking the File tab. Here you can use several common file commands or click the Options command to see a wealth of setting options that control the way PowerPoint—and you—work.

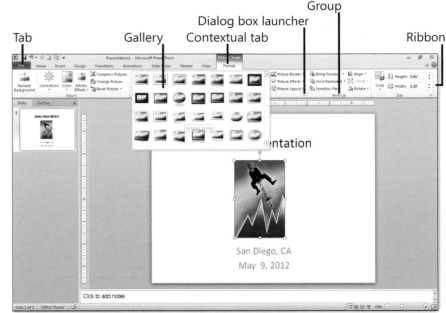

Tab   Gallery   Contextual tab   Dialog box launcher   Group   Ribbon

File tab   File menu   Options

Using the Ribbon

The ribbon is your control central in PowerPoint 2010. The default ribbon consists of nine tabs, although contextual tabs appear now and then when you work with certain types of objects or functions. The Add-Ins tab appears if you install third-party programs and features, such as Microsoft PowerPoint Presenter Tools, or a tool like the one I used to capture the screen shots for this book.

Display Tabs and Panes

(1) Click the Review tab.

(2) Click Research to open the Research pane.

(3) Click the Close button to close the pane.

ScreenTip

Try This!

You can open dialog boxes associated with groups of tools by clicking the dialog box launcher, a small arrow at the bottom-right corner of many groups on the ribbon. This displays all settings and features related to that category of functions, including some not shown on the ribbon.

④ Click the Insert tab.

⑤ Click Shapes, and then click an item in the Shapes gallery. Click anywhere on the slide, and then drag to draw the shape.

⑥ Note that the Drawing Tools, Format tab appears. This is a contextual tab.

Tip

The Add-Ins tab is where you can add programs or features that are not part of PowerPoint. You include add-in programs here by using the Options command on the File menu. For example, you can include additional presenter tools or presentation notes tools as add-ins.

Tip

Can't find a tool? Some tools, such as Preview As A Web Page, are not on the ribbon. In this case, you have to add the tools to the Quick Access Toolbar to perform the function. See the task "Customizing the Quick Access Toolbar" on page 29 for more about how to do this.

Show or Hide Enhanced ScreenTips

① Click the File tab to open the File menu.

② Click Options.

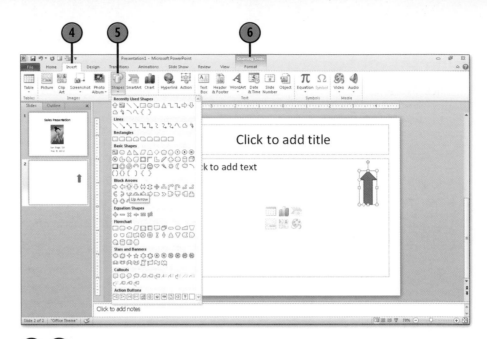

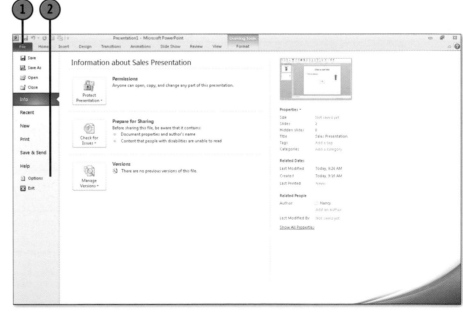

(3) Click General.

(4) Click the ScreenTip Style drop-down arrow, and choose one of the following settings:

- Show Feature Descriptions In ScreenTips, which displays larger ScreenTips with the tool button name and an explanation of its function.

- Don't Show Feature Descriptions In ScreenTips, which displays only the tool button name.

- Don't Show ScreenTips, which displays neither enhanced nor standard ScreenTips.

(5) Click OK.

(6) Place your pointer over a button on the ribbon, and the appropriate setting takes effect. (Here you see the effects of using the Show Feature Descriptions In ScreenTips setting.)

Tip ✓

When you display either type of ScreenTip, keyboard shortcuts for tool button functions are displayed (when they exist). For example, if you place your pointer over the Paste button, you see Ctrl+V in parentheses after the tool name in the ScreenTip. You can use this keyboard combination to paste an item instead of clicking the button.

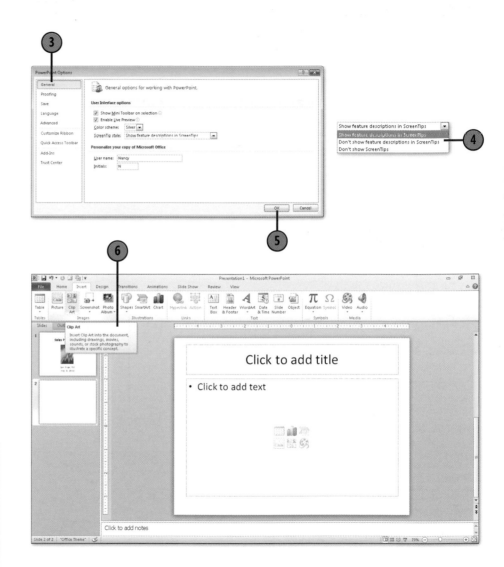

Using Microsoft Office Backstage

In PowerPoint 2010, the File tab takes you to a new command central for your documents, called Microsoft Office Backstage. This change to the Office interface in Office 2010 makes accessing often-used settings and activities such as opening, printing, and saving or publishing files easier to do using a panel of options.

Display the File Menu

① Click the File tab to open the File menu.

② Click any of the categories on the left to display detailed settings in a pane on the right.

③ Use various check boxes or settings to change the way PowerPoint functions.

④ Some choices open a dialog box in which you click OK to save changed settings.

Tip

Commands located on the File tab in PowerPoint 2010 (an area referred to as Office Backstage) are accessed via the Office button in PowerPoint 2007. From the File menu, you can make many settings that determine how certain functions in PowerPoint work, open or create documents, save files, get help, and print or publish your presentation.

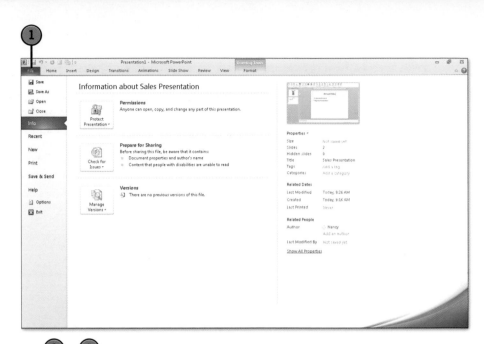

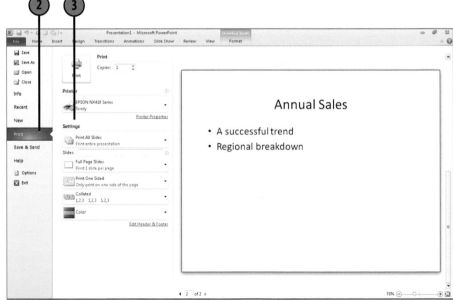

Working with Improved Picture and Video Formatting Tools

PowerPoint 2010 has easy-to-use picture formatting tools and new video formatting tools. These tools provide galleries of effects, such as a variety of contrast or color settings, for you to choose from. Here you get a look at a couple of galleries used for working with pictures. For more about working with video tools, see Section 11, "Formatting Text, Objects, and Slides," starting on page 143.

Explore the Artistic Effects and Corrections Galleries

1 Click the Insert tab.

2 Click Picture.

Try This!

The Format tab displays different tools if you insert a video. Try inserting a video from the sample video library by clicking the Insert tab and then clicking the Video button. Explore the tools available on this tab. You can learn more about these in the task "Using Video Tools," on page 162.

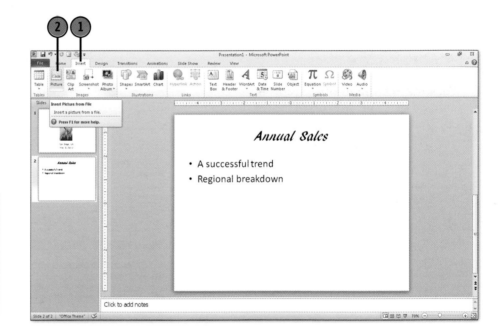

(3) Click any picture in the Pictures folder, and then click the Open button. (Use files in the Sample Pictures folder if you have none of your own.)

(4) Click the Picture Tools, Format tab if it's not displayed.

(5) Click the Artistic Effects button, and move your mouse pointer over the various effects to see them previewed on your picture object. Do the same thing with the Corrections button.

(6) Click an effect to apply it.

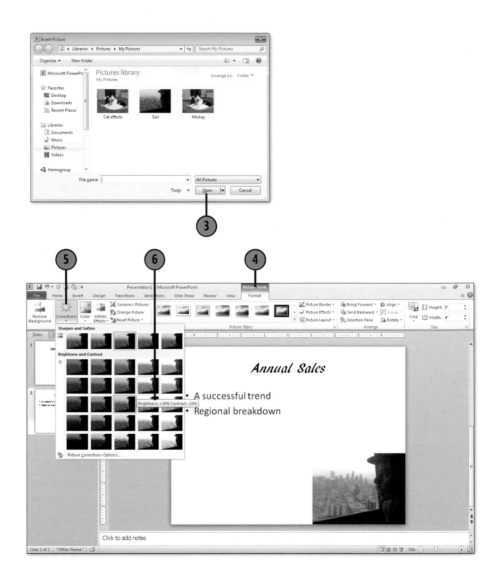

Taking Advantage of Additional Themes and SmartArt

In PowerPoint 2010, graphics are displayed in galleries that help you browse through different styles and preview how each would look in your presentation. Built-in themes and SmartArt (used to insert workflow and process charts) are designed to give your presentation visual interest.

Get a Cohesive Look with Themes

1. Click the Design tab.

2. Click the More arrow to the right of the Themes group to open the Themes gallery.

3. Move your mouse pointer over the various themes. Each in turn is previewed on your slide presentation.

4. Click a theme to apply it your entire presentation.

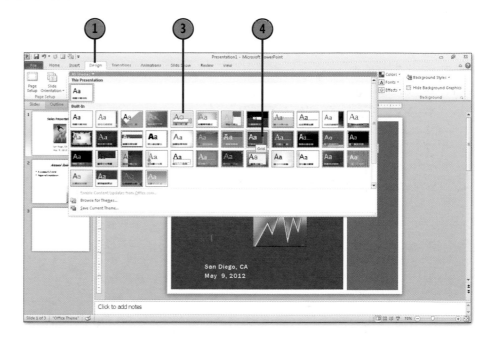

Try This!

You can modify a theme by selecting a different color, font, or effect set on the Design tab. Even if you experiment with different combinations, by using these preset design elements you can keep consistency in the various design features of your slides.

See Also

For more information about working with themes and other design elements, see Section 9, "Using Slide Layouts and Themes," starting on page 103.

5 Click the Colors button, and then move your mouse pointer over the sets of colors to see previews on your slides. Click a color scheme to apply it.

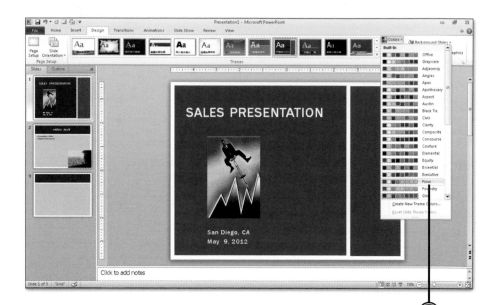

Themes were introduced in PowerPoint 2007, and Microsoft offers the option of expanding your theme horizons by visiting Office Online at *www.office.microsoft.com*. Office Online offers additional looks for your presentation that can give it extra visual excitement.

See Also

See Section 10, "Inserting Media and Drawing Objects," starting on page 113, for more about working with SmartArt objects as well as tables and various kinds of drawn objects.

Explore SmartArt

1. Click the Insert tab.

2. Click SmartArt to open the Choose A SmartArt Graphic dialog box.

3. Click a category of SmartArt in the list on the left.

4. Click an item in the gallery of SmartArt to select it.

5. Click OK. The SmartArt object appears on the slide.

6. Click in the Type Your Text Here box, and type your text.

Tip

Look at the preview of SmartArt in the Choose A SmartArt Graphic dialog box. Beneath it is a suggestion of uses for that particular SmartArt element to best communicate your message.

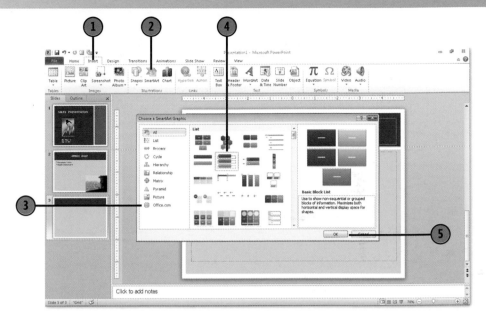

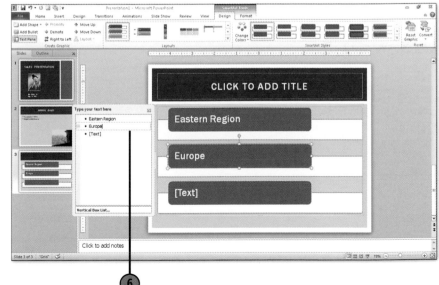

Copying Effects with Animation Painter

Animation Painter is a feature that's new to PowerPoint 2010. If you've used Format Painter, which allows you to copy formats such as font and font color from one piece of text to another, you'll understand how Animation Painter works. Animation Painter copies animation effects from one object to another, saving you the work of applying those effects time after time.

Animations with Animation Painter

1. Click on an object that has an animation applied to it to select it.
2. Click the Animations tab.
3. Click Animation Painter.
4. Click on another object to copy all animation effects from the first object to the second.

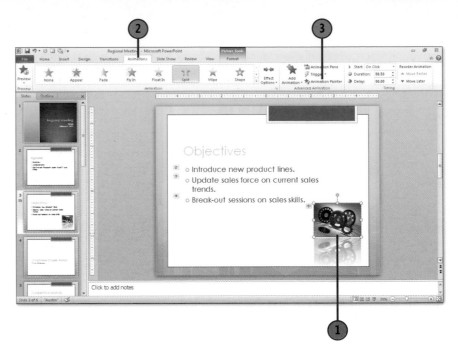

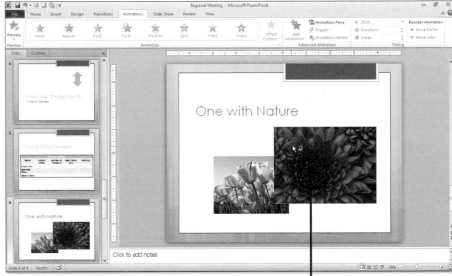

> **See Also**
>
> For more about working with Animation Painter, see the task "Using Animation Painter" on page 176.

Working with Slide Sections

Sections are a new feature in PowerPoint 2010 that allow you to divide up larger presentations so that you can find material more easily, something like headings in a long report. When you create a section and name it, its name appears in a bar that separates the slides within the section from others in the presentation. You can expand or collapse sections, as well.

Add a Section

(1) Click the Slide Sorter view button.

(2) Click to the left of the first slide in the new section.

(3) Click Section on the Home tab, and then choose Add Section.

See Also

See "Working with Sections" on page 99 for more about working with slide sections.

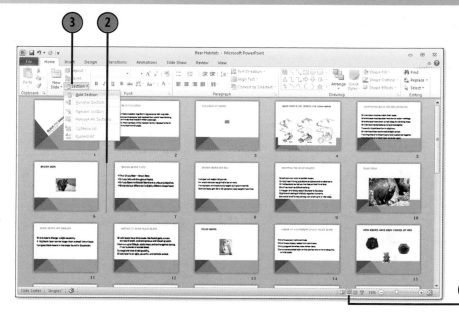

Section indicator

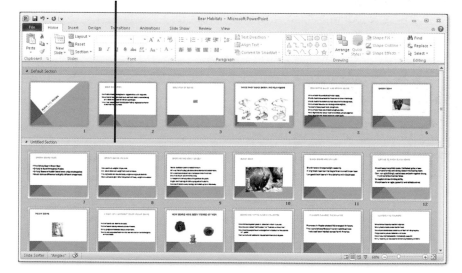

Broadcasting Slide Shows

When you broadcast a presentation, you make it available as a live presentation that others can view using their Web browsers. The process is simple, doesn't require you to have your own site to host the presentation, and is an excellent way to give a live presentation to remote viewers.

Start a Broadcast

① Click the File tab.

② Click Save & Send.

③ Click the Broadcast Slide Show link, and then click the Broadcast Slide Show button that appears.

See Also

Once you initiate and invite people to a broadcast, you can run the broadcast online. See Section 16, "Sharing a Presentation on the Web," starting on page 217, for more about working with broadcasting presentations.

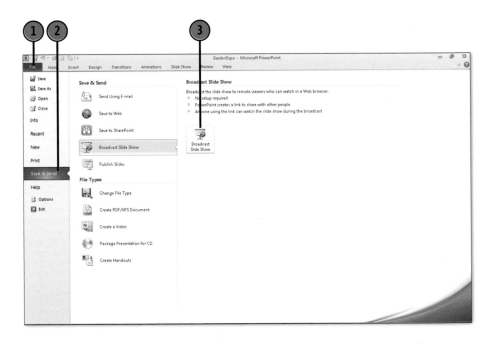

④ In the Broadcast Slide Show dialog box, click the Start Broadcast button. Enter your user ID and password if requested, and click OK. (If you don't have a Windows Live account, you can go to *www.WindowsLive.com* and sign up for one or, for more information on this feature, see Section 16, "Sharing a Presentation on the Web," starting on page 217.)

⑤ In the next dialog box that appears, click the Start Broadcast button to use the default PowerPoint Broadcast Service.

⑥ Click Copy Link to copy the Web address and paste it into an e-mail invitation yourself, or click Send In Email to simply open an e-mail message and send the link.

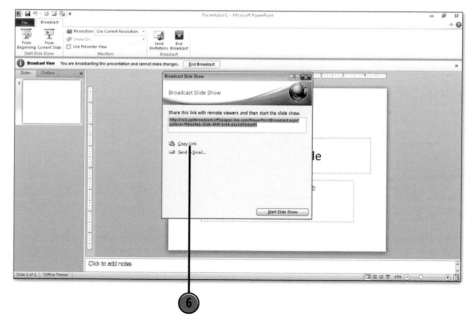

Getting Started with PowerPoint 2010

Microsoft PowerPoint 2010 sports the user interface introduced in PowerPoint 2007—with some slight changes. This interface offers a way of getting things done that's somewhat different from versions of PowerPoint prior to Microsoft Office 2007. After investing a little time getting used to the new tools and features, you'll find that this version of PowerPoint is actually easier to use.

This section is where you get your first look at PowerPoint 2010, discovering where various tools and settings reside and learning how to use features such as the ribbon and the galleries of design styles.

PowerPoint 2010 has only a single menu, the File menu, which you display by clicking the File tab. (In PowerPoint 2007, this menu was opened by using the Office button.) Other than the File menu, which offers file-management commands such as New, Open, Save, and Print, most features are available as buttons on tabs on the ribbon. In some cases, you work with panes, such as the Research pane, which are essentially like task panes in PowerPoint 2003.

Galleries of graphical selections allow you to preview how effects look on your slides or objects before you apply them. Finally, PowerPoint includes a few contextual tools that appear only when needed.

What's Where in PowerPoint 2010?

PowerPoint 2010 provides a central ribbon of tools that you access on various tabs. The tools on the tabs are broken into groups. In addition, the Quick Access Toolbar lets you place your favorite tools in one location and access functions that aren't offered through the ribbon. Some tools on the ribbon offer drop-down galleries of selections, and other tools open dialog boxes for making detailed settings.

Tabs   Dialog box launcher   Group   Ribbon

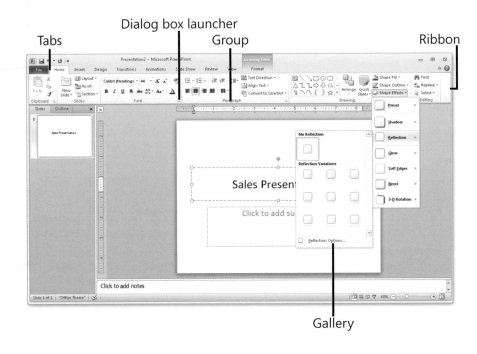

Gallery

You access the File menu by clicking the File tab. Here you can choose several common file commands or click the Options command to see a wealth of setting options that control the way PowerPoint—and you—work.

File menu

Contextual tab

File tab

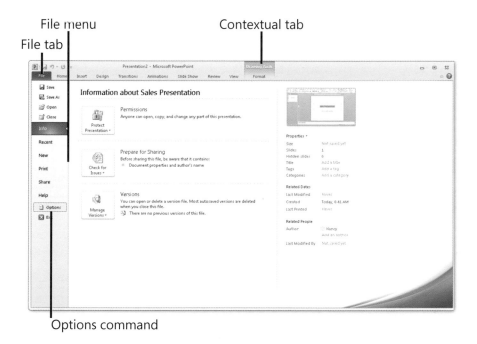

Options command

Using the Ribbon

The ribbon is your control central in PowerPoint 2010. The default ribbon consists of nine tabs, although contextual tabs appear now and then when you work with certain types of objects or functions. An additional tab, Add-Ins, appears if you install third-party programs and features, such as Microsoft PowerPoint Presenter Tools, or a tool like the one I used to capture the screen shots for this book.

Display Tabs and Panes

1. Click the Review tab.

2. Click Research to open the Research pane.

3. Click the Close button to close the pane.

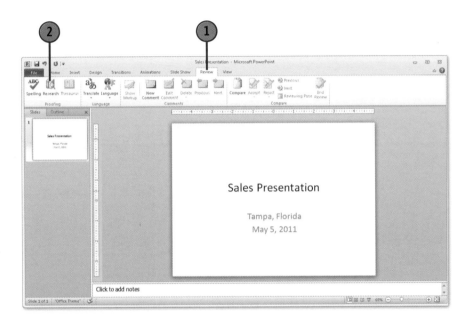

> **Tip**
>
> The Add-Ins tab is where you can add programs or features that are not part of PowerPoint. You include add-in programs here by using the Options command on the File menu. For example, you can include additional presenter tools or presentation notes tools as add-ins.

④ Click the Insert tab.

⑤ Click the Shapes button, and then click an item in the Shapes group. Click anywhere on the slide, and then drag to draw the shape.

⑥ Note that the Drawing Tools, Format tab appears. This is a contextual tab.

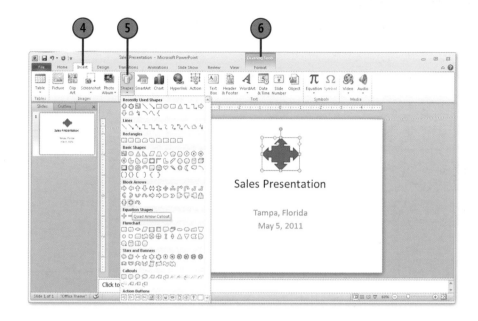

Try This!

You can open dialog boxes associated with groups of tools by clicking the dialog box launcher, the small arrow at the bottom-right corner of many groups on the ribbon. This displays additional settings and features related to the ribbon functions.

Tip

Can't find a tool? Some tools, such as Preview As A Web Page, are not on the ribbon. In this case, you have to add the tools to the Quick Access Toolbar to perform the function. See the task "Customizing the Quick Access Toolbar" on page 29 for more about how to do this.

Show or Hide Enhanced ScreenTips

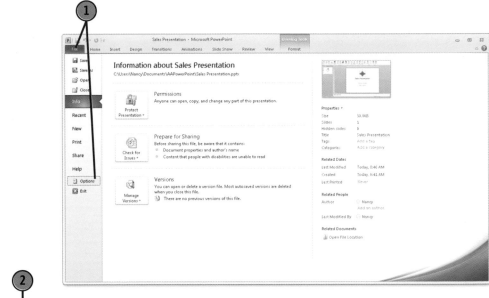

1. Choose Options from the File menu.

2. Click General.

3. Click the ScreenTip Style drop-down arrow, and choose one of the following settings:

   - Show Feature Descriptions In ScreenTips displays larger ScreenTips with the tool button name and an explanation of its function.

   - Don't Show Feature Descriptions In ScreenTips displays only the tool button name.

   - Don't Show ScreenTips displays neither enhanced nor standard ScreenTips.

4. Click OK.

5. Place your mouse pointer over a button on the ribbon and the appropriate setting takes effect. (Here you see the effects of choosing the Show Feature Descriptions In ScreenTips setting.)

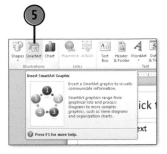

Tip

When you display either type of ScreenTip, keyboard shortcuts for tool button functions are also displayed (when they exist). For example, if you move your mouse pointer over the Paste button, you see Ctrl+V in parentheses after the tool name in the ScreenTip. You can use this keyboard combination to paste an item instead of clicking the button.

Working with the Mini Toolbar

Everybody who has ever worked on any kind of document, from a word-processed letter to a PowerPoint presentation, knows that formatting text is one of the most frequent tasks they perform. That is perhaps why Microsoft created the Mini

toolbar. When you select text, a small floating toolbar appears right next to the text itself. You can easily click on tools such as Bold, Italic, or Font Size without having to move your mouse pointer up to the ribbon and back to the text again.

Display the Mini Toolbar

① Choose Options from the File menu.

② Click General.

③ Select the Show Mini Toolbar On Selection check box.

④ Click OK.

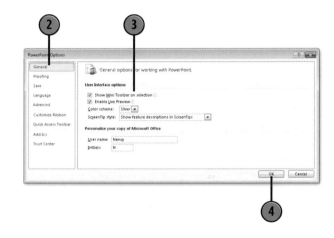

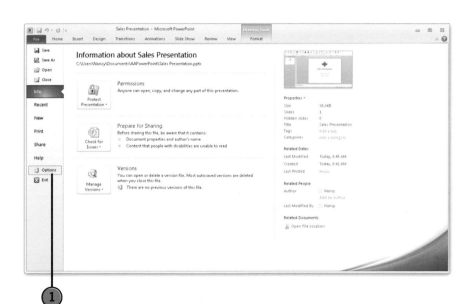

⑤ Select text on a slide. The Mini toolbar appears.

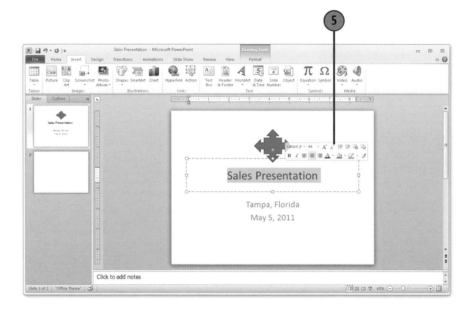

See Also

For more information about working with
text formatting tools that appear both
on the Home tab of the ribbon and on
the Mini toolbar, see Section 11, "Formatting Text, Objects, and Slides," starting on
page 143.

Tip

The Mini toolbar is somewhat translucent when you first select
text; you have to move your pointer to it to get a solid image
of the tool buttons on it. If you move the mouse pointer away
from the toolbar, you have to select the text again to make the
toolbar appear.

Customizing the Quick Access Toolbar

The idea behind the interface that Microsoft Office 2007 introduced is that the most commonly used tools are present on the ribbon rather than buried in dialog boxes, and the tools you use less often, though accessible, aren't part of the main interface by default. Sometimes the only way to access a function you might have used in previous versions of PowerPoint is to place a command on the Quick Access Toolbar. By default this toolbar contains only the Save, Undo, and Redo commands, but you can add as many commands as you want.

Add Buttons to the Quick Access Toolbar

① Choose Options from the File menu.

Caution

Although you can add many tools to the toolbar, don't overdo it. Only add the tools you use most often, or add a tool to use a particular function and then remove it to clear clutter off the toolbar.

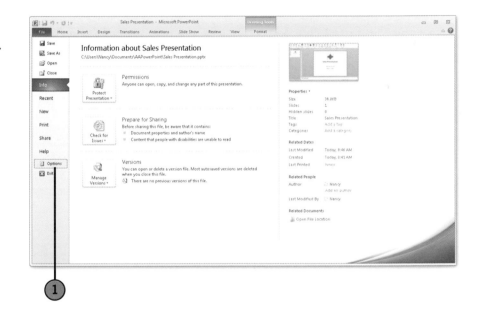

② Click Quick Access Toolbar.

③ In the Choose Commands From list, click the arrow and select a category of tools, or simply scroll down and choose the Commands Not In The Ribbon category.

④ Click a command in the list on the left, and then click the Add button to add it to the toolbar. Repeat this step for all the commands you want to add.

⑤ Click OK.

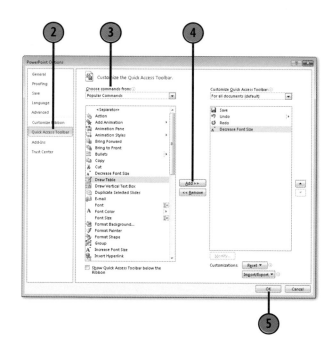

The tools are added to the toolbar.

If you fill up your Quick Access Toolbar and want to put it back the way it was when you first installed PowerPoint, go to the PowerPoint Options dialog box, select Quick Access Toolbar, and click Reset. The default tool settings are restored.

You can use the same procedure to add tools to the ribbon, except that in step 2, you select Customize Ribbon instead of Quick Access Toolbar. However, I suggest that you avoid customizing the ribbon extensively because other people using your computer won't be familiar with what you've done and Help files will reflect only the default ribbon settings, which could be confusing.

Remove or Rearrange Tools

1. Choose Options from the File menu.

2. Click Quick Access Toolbar.

3. Click an item in the list on the right.

4. Click Remove to remove it from the toolbar.

5. Click Move Up or Move Down to rearrange the tools.

6. Click OK to save your settings.

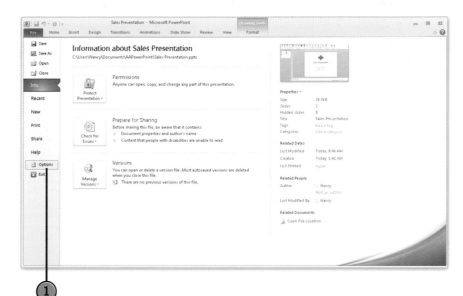

Try This!

You can change the Quick Access Toolbar settings for just the currently opened document, not for all documents. When you are in the Quick Access Toolbar window in the PowerPoint Options dialog box, click the arrow on the Customize Quick Access Toolbar list and choose the name of the presentation for which you want to save the changes.

Tip

If you want to add some space between sets of tools on the Quick Access Toolbar, simply click the item labeled <Separator> at the top of the list on the left of the Quick Access Toolbar window, and then click Add.

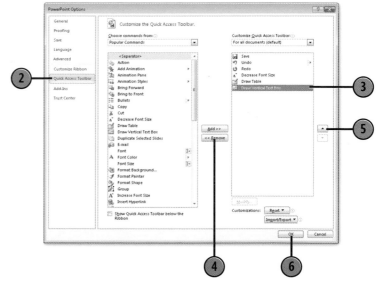

Working with Design Elements

Several features introduced in PowerPoint 2007 relate to how graphics are displayed and created, so if you have worked only with older versions of PowerPoint, this section gives you a quick preview of those features. Galleries of graphical elements help you browse through different styles and preview how each looks in your presentation. Themes and Quick Styles are designed to give your presentation a cohesive and consistent look with predesigned combinations of colors, graphics, and fonts. Finally, SmartArt is a feature that allows you to easily create various types of diagrams and add text to them.

Preview Design Elements with Galleries

① Click a placeholder on a slide, enter some text, and select the text.

② Click the Format tab.

③ Click the More arrow at the bottom right of the WordArt Styles gallery.

④ Move your mouse pointer over various WordArt styles. You can see each style previewed on the selected text. Click a style to apply it.

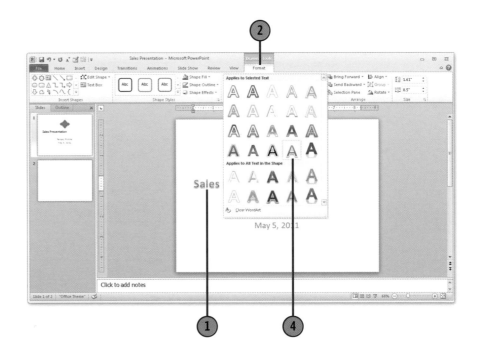

Tip

Several galleries exist on tabs that don't appear until you insert certain types of objects, such as pictures or drawings. Although the Format tab contains an Insert Shapes group, there is also a Shapes gallery on the Insert tab, which you can use to draw shapes on your slides when the Format tab isn't available.

(5) Click the Home tab, and then click the arrow on the Font list.

(6) Move your mouse pointer down the list of fonts. You can see each font previewed on the selected text. Click a font to apply it.

Try This!

You can preview font sizes on selected text. With text selected, click the arrow on the Font Size list and move your mouse pointer down the list of sizes. Each is previewed on your text.

See Also

For more information about WordArt and other drawing objects, see Section 10, "Inserting Media and Drawing Objects," starting on page 113.

Get a Cohesive Look with Themes

1. Click the Design tab.

2. Click the down arrow to the right of the Themes gallery. The gallery scrolls to the next row.

3. Move your mouse pointer over the various themes. You see each one previewed on your slide presentation.

4. Click a theme to apply it to your entire presentation.

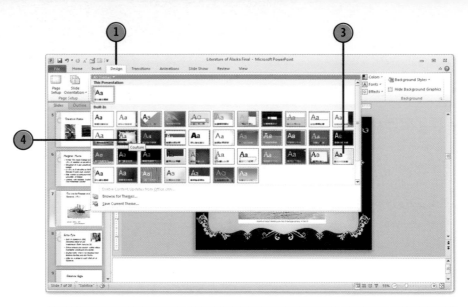

Try This!

You can modify a theme by selecting a different color, font, or effect set on the Design tab. Even if you experiment with different combinations, by using these preset design elements you can keep consistency in the various design features of your slides.

See Also

For more information about working with themes and other design elements, see Section 9, "Using Slide Layouts and Themes," starting on page 103.

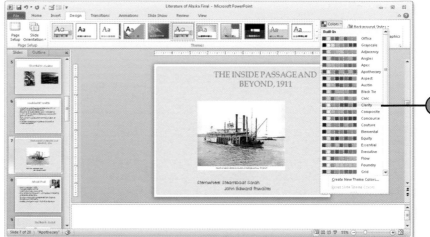

5. Click the Colors button and move your mouse pointer over the sets of colors to see them previewed on your slides. Click a color scheme to apply it.

Tip

You can expand the Theme gallery to view all available themes rather than scrolling through line by line. Click the More button (a down arrow with a line above it) to expand the gallery.

Work with SmartArt

(1) Click the Insert tab.

(2) Click the SmartArt button to open the Choose A SmartArt Graphic dialog box.

(3) Click a category of SmartArt in the list on the left.

(4) Click an item in the gallery of SmartArt to select it.

(5) Click OK.

(6) Click in the Type Your Text Here box, and then type your text.

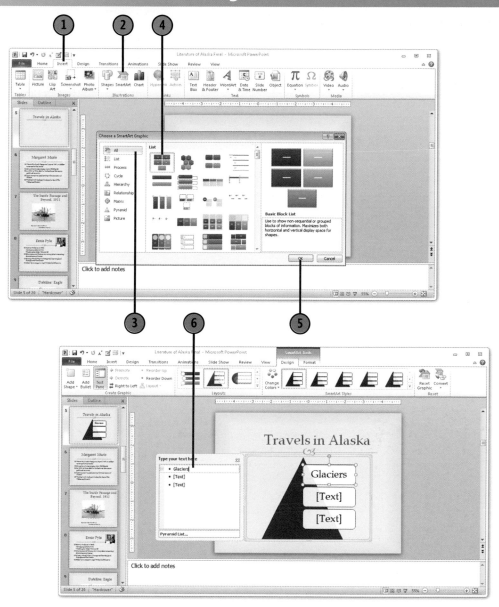

Tip

Look at the preview of SmartArt in the Choose A SmartArt Graphic dialog box. Beneath it is a suggestion of uses for that particular SmartArt element to best communicate your message.

See Also

See Section 10 for more about working with SmartArt objects as well as tables and various kinds of drawn objects.

4

Creating Presentations

When you start a new job, you typically spend the first day getting acquainted with colleagues and finding your way around the office before you get to work. In the same way, whether you want to create a lengthy, elaborate, animated presentation with sound and graphics or a simple presentation consisting of a bulleted list and a handful of slides, your first steps are to learn how to open a blank presentation and to understand the basic structure of a standard Microsoft PowerPoint 2010 presentation.

You can open a blank presentation, open presentations you have previously created and saved, or create presentations based on templates that provide prebuilt design features. After you open a file, you can enter content for a presentation. Then, if you make changes, you need to know how to save those changes and close the presentation.

As you wander around PowerPoint, you get to know the different views you use to accomplish various tasks. When you open a presentation, it opens in Normal view, where you see three panes showing a slide/outline display, the current slide, and an area for notes.

Slide Sorter view is where you go to organize slides. When you want to see your slide show in action, use Slide Show view.

Creating a Presentation

PowerPoint offers a few options for how you get started with a new presentation. For example, if you want a single blank slide with the default layout and design elements, you can open a blank presentation. But if you want to get a head start on your presentation, consider basing it on an existing presentation that contains some elements you want to reuse or applying one of the templates that come with PowerPoint.

Open a Blank Presentation

① With PowerPoint running, choose New from the File menu to display the New Presentation window.

② Click Create to open a new presentation based on the default Blank Presentation template.

Tip

If you're more comfortable using a keyboard shortcut to open a file, you can. Simply press Ctrl+O to display the Open dialog box or Ctrl+N to open a new blank presentation. You should note, however, that keyboard shortcuts are not displayed on the File menu in PowerPoint 2010, as they are in some previous versions.

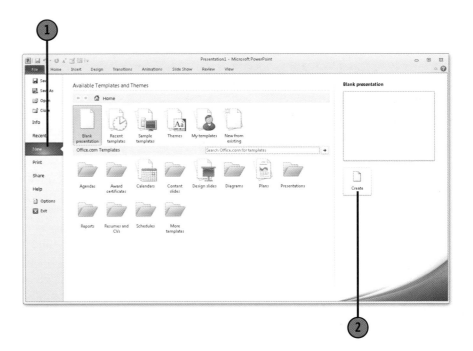

Open a Presentation Based on an Existing Presentation

(1) With PowerPoint running, choose New from the File menu to display the New Presentation window.

(2) Click New From Existing.

(3) Click the items in the navigation pane of the dialog box that appears to browse the drives and folders of your computer or network.

(4) Double-click a folder to open it. Continue to double-click folders in the right pane until you find the file you want.

(5) Click the document file to select it.

(6) Click Create New to open a new presentation based on the presentation you selected.

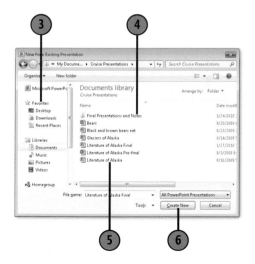

See Also

For information about saving files, see "Saving and Closing a PowerPoint Presentation" on page 49.

Tip

Be sure to save the file you just created to preserve its contents. Be sure to save it with a name different from the file it is based on to ensure that you don't overwrite the original file.

Open a Template

① With PowerPoint running, choose New from the File menu to display the New Presentation window.

② If you are online, you can click the Presentations category in the Office.com Templates area of the window to display categories of templates available from Office Online.

③ Click a category, select a template, and then click the Download button to download the template.

④ If you don't want to use an online template, click Sample Templates to view the templates installed on your computer when you installed PowerPoint.

⑤ Click a template to see a preview on the right side of the window.

⑥ Click a template to select it, and then click Create.

Tip

If you previously saved a template, you can use the My Templates selection in the Available Templates And Themes list to locate and open one.

See Also

Any template you apply to your presentation is accessible by clicking Themes on the Design tab. For information about applying themes to slides, see "Apply a Slide Theme" on page 108.

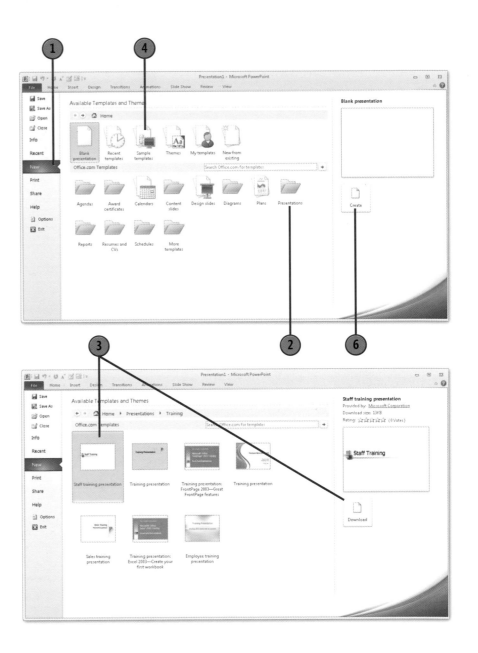

Finding and Opening Existing Presentations

Very often, you use several work sessions to complete a presentation. Perhaps you enter slide text in one sitting, tweak the arrangement of graphics and colors in another, and still later edit what you created to incorporate others' feedback or to proof for spelling errors. To open an existing presentation, you can use the following steps.

Open a Presentation

① With PowerPoint running, choose Open from the File menu to display the Open dialog box.

② Click in the navigation pane on the left to browse the drives and folders on your computer or network.

③ Double-click a folder to open it and display files in the right pane. Continue to double-click folders until you find the file you want.

④ You might need to specify the file type for the document you want to locate; All PowerPoint Presentations is the default format. Only documents saved in the specified file format are displayed in the file list.

⑤ Click a file, and then click Open.

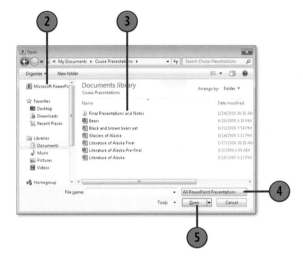

Tip

You can use the buttons along the left of the Open dialog box to find a file more quickly. For example, if you just downloaded the file recently, click the Downloads button; if the file is stored in a shared folder on a network, click the Network button to locate it; and so on.

Tip

If you used a file recently, choose Recent from the File menu, and just click one of the listed files to open it.

Moving Among Views

PowerPoint 2010 offers several views that let you focus on different aspects of your presentation. Four of the views—Normal, Slide Sorter, Reading view, and Slide Show—can be accessed from buttons on the status bar located along the bottom of the PowerPoint window; another view, Notes Page, is accessed through the View tab. Note that these buttons do not appear when your presentation is in Slide Show view. You must exit the slide show to use them. You learn more about how each view is used in the following sections.

Slide Show view

View tab

Slide Sorter View

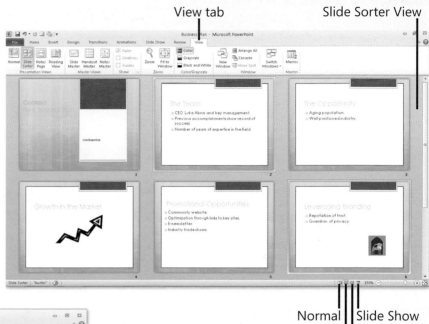

Normal | Slide Show

Slide Sorter

Reading View

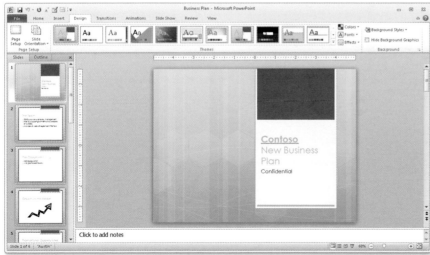

Normal view

Sizing Panes in Normal View

You do most of your work building your presentation in Normal view. It consists of three panes: the Slides/Outline pane gives you access to tabs that provide an overview of your presentation; the Notes pane is where you enter speaker notes to help you when you give your presentation; and the Slide pane is where you work on the design of an individual slide. You can temporarily remove the Slides/Outline or Notes panes, or you can resize them to focus on one aspect of your presentation.

Resize a Pane

①   Move your mouse pointer over the edge of the Slides/Outline or Notes pane until the pointer turns into two lines with double arrows.

②   Drag the pane divider in the appropriate direction to make the pane larger or smaller.

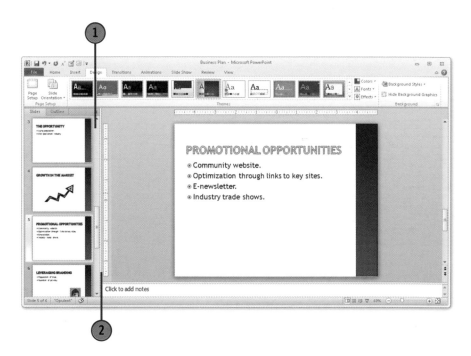

If you drag a pane divider until the pane disappears, the divider is still visible. You can drag the divider to display the pane again. Note that the Outline/Slide pane on the left of Normal view can be resized to a maximum width of about 4 inches.

You can change how large the slide preview appears in the Slide pane without resizing the pane by dragging the zoom slider at the bottom of the PowerPoint window. To refit the slide to the Slide pane in Normal view after you change its zoom setting, click the Fit Slide To Current Window button, located to the right of the zoom slider. The Fit Slide To Current Window button does not appear in any other view.

Close and Redisplay the Slides/ Outline Pane

(1) Click the Close button on the Slides/ Outline pane to hide it.

(2) Click Normal on the View tab to redisplay the pane.

See Also

For information about working with the Slides tab, see Section 6, "Building a Presentation," starting on page 67.

For information about working with the Outline feature, see Section 7, "Building a Presentation Outline," starting on page 81.

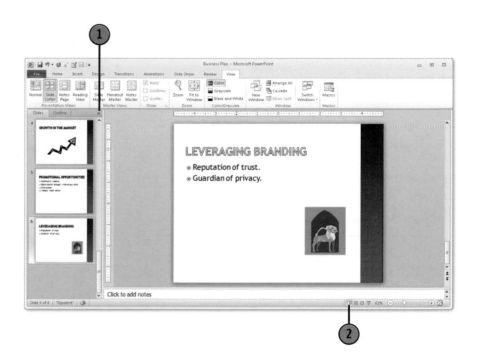

Try This!

Take advantage of the ability to hide and resize panes to make your work easier. If you need to focus on slide design rather than on entering slide text, close the Slides/Outline pane or make it smaller. If you want to quickly enter text in an outline format for many slides, enlarge the Slides/Outline pane to make the Outline tab larger and the text easier to read.

Viewing Multiple Slides with Slide Sorter

After you create several slides, you might want to take your focus off an individual slide and look at your presentation as a whole. The best view for this task is Slide Sorter view, which displays all your slides as thumbnails placed in sequence from left to right. If you have many slides, they are arranged in rows. In this view, it's easy to locate a slide, rearrange slides to organize your slide show, or duplicate or delete slides.

Display Slide Sorter View

① Click the Slide Sorter button to display the view.

Display More Slides in Slide Sorter

① Drag the slider on the zoom tool to the left to make the thumbnails smaller and fit more slides on the screen. Drag to the right to make the thumbnails larger, fitting fewer on the screen.

> **See Also**
>
> You can do more than view slides in Slide Sorter view. You can delete, duplicate, hide, and reorder slides, as well as preview animations and more. See Section 8, "Managing and Viewing Slides," starting on page 91 for more features of this handy view.

This icon indicates that animation is applied to a slide.

Slide numbers are displayed beneath each slide.

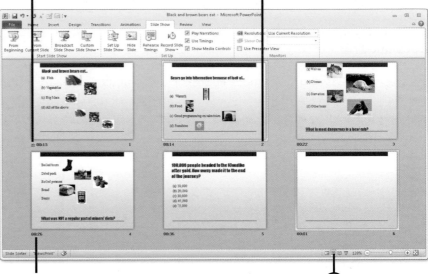

Slide timings appear beneath slides if you have rehearsed the presentation and saved timings.

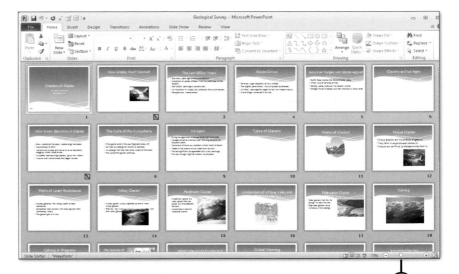

Running a Presentation in Slide Show View

Slide Show is the view you use to run your presentation in full-screen mode. If you have your computer connected to an LCD or television monitor, your audience can view your presentation using a larger screen format than is available on your computer.

Slide Show view has several useful tools for navigating through your show, including a pen feature that lets you annotate your slides as you show them. You can even save your annotations at the end of the show.

The new Reading view is essentially a slide show view that is useful for people viewing your presentation on a computer rather than a large screen. This view has similar navigation options.

Start a Slide Show and Advance Slides

① Click the Slide Show view button to display the slide show starting with the currently selected slide.

② Press the Left arrow key to move back one slide, or press the Right arrow key to move forward one slide.

End a Slide Show

1 With a presentation in Slide Show view, press Esc on your keyboard to end the slide show and return to the view displayed when you started the presentation (Normal or Slide Sorter).

2 If you created any annotations while running the show, a dialog box appears asking whether you want to save your annotations. Click Keep or Discard.

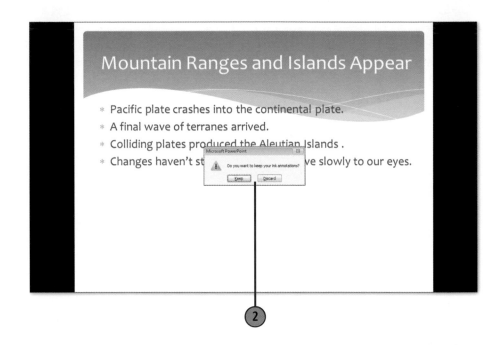

Tip

You can end a slide show at any point, whether you've reached the last slide or not, by using the method described here. If, however, you finish running through the slides in your show and reach the end, you see a message that the show is over. If you see that message, press any key to close the slide show.

See Also

For information about using different methods to navigate through a slide show, including your mouse, onscreen buttons, and the Slide Show menu, see Section 14, "Running a Presentation," starting on page 195. For information about setting up the way a slide show runs, see Section 13, "Finalizing Your Slide Show," starting on page 179.

Saving and Closing a PowerPoint Presentation

As you work on a presentation, you should save it periodically so that you don't run the risk of losing any of your work in the event of a computer crash or other problem. You should also save any changes you want to keep before closing a file.

Save a Presentation

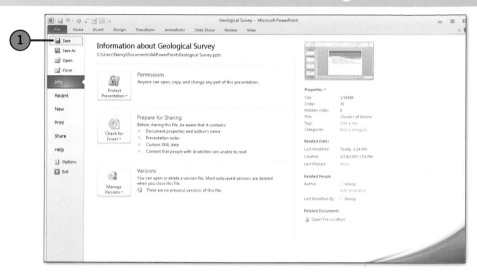

1. Choose Save from the File menu to display the Save As dialog box.

2. If you don't want to save the presentation to the default folder, select another drive or folder.

3. Type a name for the document of up to 255 characters; you cannot use the characters * : < > | " \ or /.

4. To save the document in a format other than the default PowerPoint file format (.pptx), select a different format.

5. Click Save.

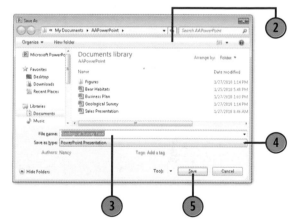

Try This!

If you want to save a previously saved presentation with a new name, perhaps to use as the basis for another presentation, choose Save As from the File menu. Type a new file name and, if you want to, locate another folder in which to save the file. Click Save, and you save a copy of the presentation with a new name.

Tip

To quickly save any changes to a previously saved document, simply click the Save button on the Quick Access Toolbar. The file is saved without displaying the Save As dialog box.

Tip

You can now save a presentation in PDF format, which allows users of Adobe Acrobat or Adobe Reader to view it. Simply choose PDF in step 4 of this task to use this feature.

Close a Presentation

1. Click the Save button to be sure that all changes have been saved.

2. Click the Close button to close the file and PowerPoint.

Try This!

If you want to close an open presentation without closing PowerPoint—for example, to begin a new blank presentation—choose Close from the File menu.

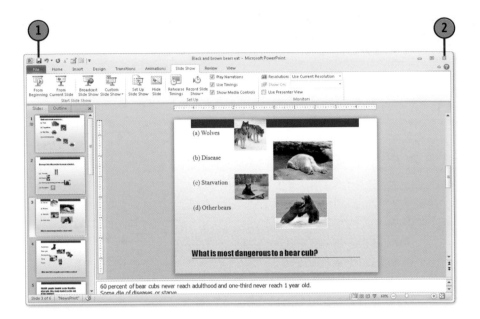

Tip

You can also close PowerPoint by choosing Exit from the File menu.

Getting Help

PowerPoint 2010 includes both offline Help, in the form of a searchable database of information, and online Help, which takes you to a Microsoft Web site. Learning how to use

PowerPoint Help enables you to solve small problems that you run into and to delve deeper into PowerPoint features.

Use Help

1 Click the Microsoft PowerPoint Help button to display the PowerPoint Help window.

2 Enter a search term and click Search.

3 Click the Show Table Of Contents button for a list of offline Help topics.

4 Click Home to go to the main listing of topics at any time.

5 Click the Print button to print the currently displayed topic.

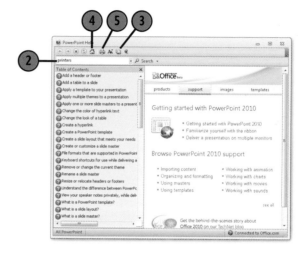

Caution

If you want to keep the Help window visible as you work in your document, click the Keep On Top button before clicking within the document.

Tip

Often, Help search results include links to other information. These links appear in blue. Click one, and you are taken to a Web page or other document where you can find related or additional information.

5

Working with Slide Masters

One of the hallmarks of a good presentation is a uniform look and feel. To achieve that consistency, you can use themes and color schemes built right into PowerPoint. (For more about these features, see Section 9, "Using Slide Layouts and Themes," starting on page 103.) But you might want to use other elements consistently from slide to slide, such as a company logo, and having to add these elements again and again—slide by slide—can be cumbersome.

That's where masters come in. A master allows you to add a graphic, modify the text formatting or slide layout, or add a global footer. Then, whatever you add to the master appears on every slide.

Masters are flexible as well. If you want one section of your presentation to use a master element or two, but in another section you want to introduce a change, you can use more than one master in your presentation to do so.

You can work with three types of masters in PowerPoint: a slide master, a handout master, and a notes master. Keep in mind that any changes you make to individual slides override the settings on masters.

Understanding How Slide Masters Work

Slide masters start out with a set of slide layouts defined by the currently applied theme. That theme determines the font treatment, placement and size of placeholders, background graphics, animation, and color scheme. You can make changes to any of the layouts in a slide master so that any time you apply one of those layouts to a slide, whatever is on that layout in the master appears automatically. You can use the Edit Master tools on the Slide Master tab to add a master set or add a new layout to an existing master set. Use Edit Theme tools on the Slide Master tab to change formatting for the text on your slides.

Slide Master tab

Master graphic

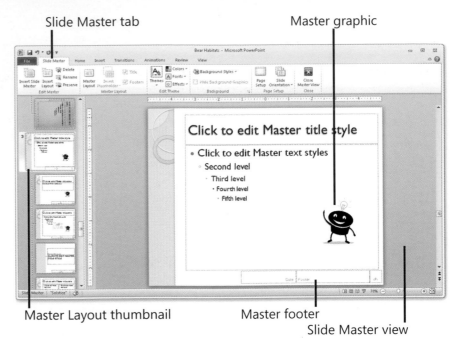

Master Layout thumbnail

Master footer

Slide Master view

Individual slide

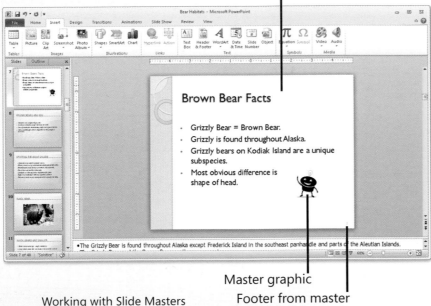

Master graphic

Footer from master

Making Changes to a Slide Master

Within Slide Master view, you can work with font formats and bullet list styles, insert text or text boxes, add graphics, or rearrange elements of any slide layout. (You learn more about how to take these actions in Sections 6, 9, and 10.) You make these changes much as you do in Normal view. However, any changes you make in Slide Master view are reflected on every slide to which the changed layout is applied. If you want to apply changes to all slides except the Title Slide layout, make those changes to the Master Layout at the top of the layout thumbnails.

Display and Navigate Masters

① Click the View tab, and choose Slide Master from the Master Views group.

② Drag the vertical scrollbar on the left pane to view more layouts in the master set.

③ Drag the divider between panes if you want to see more or less of either pane.

④ To close Slide Master view, click the Close Master View button or click the Normal, Slide Sorter, Notes Page, or Reading View button.

Try This!

Make changes to the slide master, and then save the presentation as a template (.potx). You can then base future presentations on that template. That way, you can set up your company standard logo, colors, and so on only once and then use the template again and again.

Tip

You can use the zoom slider in the bottom-right corner of the PowerPoint 2010 window to zoom in on and out of the currently displayed layout in Slide Master view's Slide pane.

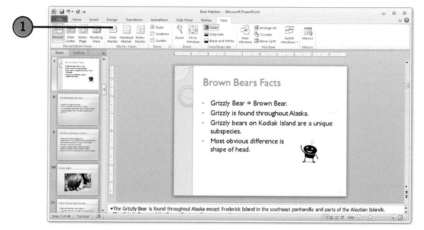

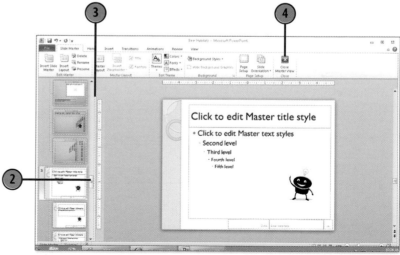

Insert Footer Information

1 With Slide Master view displayed, click a footer placeholder to select it. Note that one placeholder contains the current date by default.

2 Enter whatever text you want in the placeholder. If you want to move the footer placeholder, drag it to a new location on the slide.

3 A slide number element is included at the bottom right of slides. If you don't want to use it, select it and press the Delete key to get rid of it, or if you want to use the element but prefer a different location, drag it to another location on the slide.

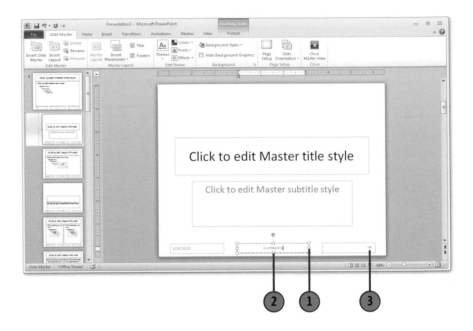

Tip

If you delete a footer placeholder in a layout and then want to put it back the way it was, in Slide Master view, click the layout to select it, click the Slide Master tab, and then select the Footers check box. All the original footer placeholders are reinstated.

Tip

The date footer is set to update automatically to reflect the current date when you run the presentation. If you don't want to display the current date, delete the current date from the placeholder, and type a specific fixed date for each slide layout where you want it to appear. If you prefer that this footer reflect the date and time, or simply the time, use the Date & Time button on the Insert tab to do so.

Work with Master Graphics

(1) With the slide master displayed, select the layout on which you want to place the graphic (for example, the title slide or a content slide), and click the Insert tab. If you want to insert the graphic on every layout except the Title Slide layout, click the top-level slide master.

(2) Use the controls in the Illustrations or Images group to insert a master graphic in your presentation:

- Click to insert a picture.

- Click to insert clip art.

- Click to insert a chart.

(3) When you have inserted a graphic on the slide master, you can resize it or drag it to wherever you want to position it.

See Also

See Section 10, "Inserting Media and Drawing Objects," starting on page 113, for more about inserting pictures, clip art, and charts in your presentation; see "Resizing Objects" on page 154 for more about changing the size of objects.

Caution

When you place a master graphic, you typically put it in a corner of a slide so that it doesn't overlap placeholder text or elements such as large tables. Still, if you use a graphic on every slide, the odds are that it will overlap some object on a few slides in the presentation. Be sure to check for this, and then move the graphic or use the procedure in the task "Omit Master Graphics on Individual Slides" on page 59 to remove the graphic on those individual slides.

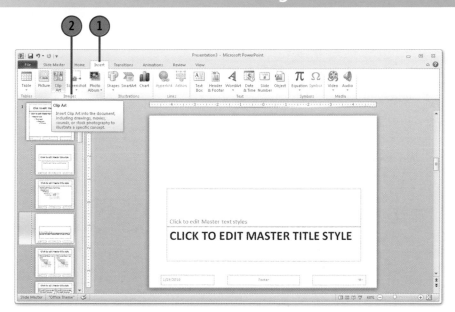

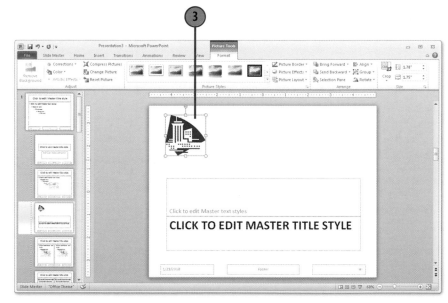

Add a Layout

(1) With Slide Master view displayed, click the Slide Master tab, and choose Insert Layout.

(2) On the new Custom Layout slide that appears, make any changes you want to the layout, such as the following:

- Click Insert Placeholder to insert a new placeholder for any type of content.

- Click an existing placeholder and press Delete.

- Drag a placeholder to a new position on the slide.

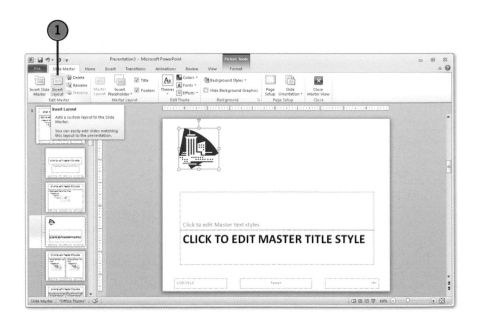

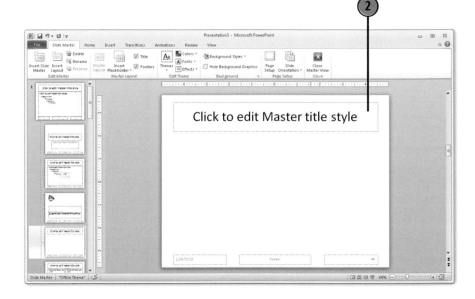

Omit Master Graphics on Individual Slides

1. With the slide displayed in Normal view, click the Design tab on the ribbon.

2. In the Background group, select the Hide Background Graphics check box.

3. Repeat these two steps for any other slides on which you want to omit master graphics.

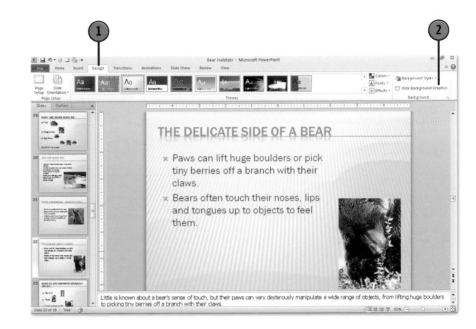

Try This!

What if you have more than one master graphic and you want to omit one but not the others from an individual slide? You have to do this manually. Use the steps here to omit all master graphics, and then insert the ones you want to use on the current slide one by one.

Adding and Deleting Master Sets

You can apply multiple themes to a single presentation. A set of master layouts is created whenever you apply an additional theme template to your presentation. When you apply another theme to some of your slides, another set of thumbnails is displayed in the left pane of the Slide Master view. You can also insert a new blank master and then apply effects to it one by

one to make a custom master or duplicate a master and then make changes to it.

If you have no more need for a master, you can delete it, or you can rename it (for example, Company Logo Master) to make it easy to identify.

Rename a Master

1 With Slide Master view displayed, click the Master Layout slide for the master you want to rename.

2 On the Slide Master tab, click Rename in the Edit Master group.

3 In the Rename Layout dialog box, type a new name and click Rename.

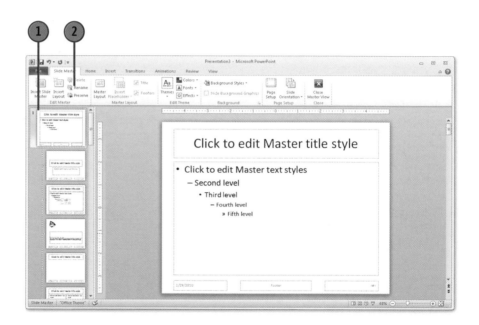

Caution

Don't overdo it! The whole point of themes is that they instantly apply a consistent look and feel to your presentation. Mixing and matching too many themes creates a messy and cluttered-looking presentation. A couple of themes is typically the most you should use in any presentation to designate major sections or changes of mood.

Tip

Consider adding presentations including custom masters to a centralized online library of presentations in Microsoft SharePoint. By setting up a SharePoint site, you can build slide libraries and sets of templates everybody in your company can use to streamline presentation creation.

Delete a Master

① With Slide Master view displayed, click the Master Layout slide for the master you want to delete.

② Click the Home tab.

③ Click Delete in the Slides group.

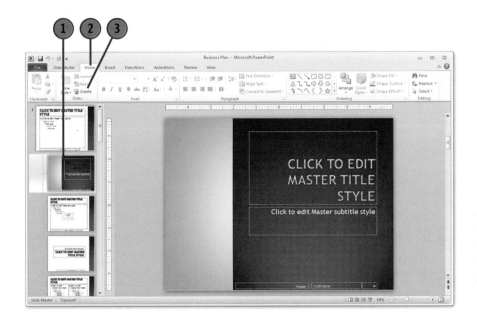

Caution

If you delete a master from Slide Master, you can't undo the delete. You have to insert the master again by applying a theme to slides or by using the Insert Slide Master button on the Slide Master tab when Slide Master view is displayed. Note that you cannot delete the Title Slide master.

See Also

For more information about applying themes to your presentation, see "Apply a Slide Theme" on page 108.

Insert Additional Masters

1. To insert a blank master, with Slide Master view displayed, click the Slide Master tab, and then click Insert Slide Master in the Edit Master group.

2. To insert an additional theme in your presentation, click Themes in the Edit Theme group, and then click the theme you want from the gallery that appears.

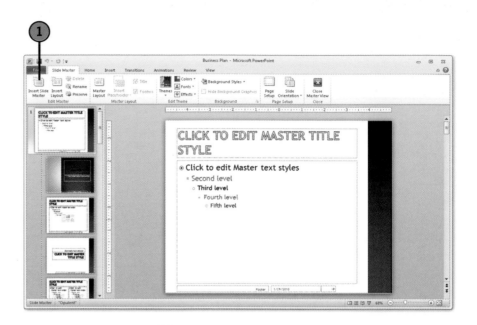

Tip

You can also simply apply a theme to your presentation or to some of the slides in your presentation in Normal view. That theme is automatically added as a new set of masters in Slide Master view.

Working with Handout and Notes Masters

Handouts are essentially a printing option for PowerPoint. You can print one, two, three, four, six, or nine slides on a page and hand out those pages to your audience to follow along with your presentation or to take with them as a reminder of key points. In the handout master, you can enter up to two headers and two footers, rearrange or delete placeholders, set the orientation of the handouts, and set the number of slides to print on a page.

Notes can be printed for the benefit of the person making the presentation, providing a handy reference while presenting. Notes consist of a slide along with an area for notes and placeholders for header and footer text. You can enter notes in the Notes pane of Normal view. The notes master allows you to arrange the placement of the various elements on the Notes page globally.

Work with Handout Master

① On the View tab, click Handout Master in the Master Views group.

② Do any of the following:

- Click in a placeholder and enter text or replace the date or slide number element already there.

- Drag a placeholder to a new location.

- Click to remove any of the four placeholders from handouts.

③ Click the Handout Masters contextual tab and then click Slide Orientation or Handout Orientation, and choose Portrait or Landscape.

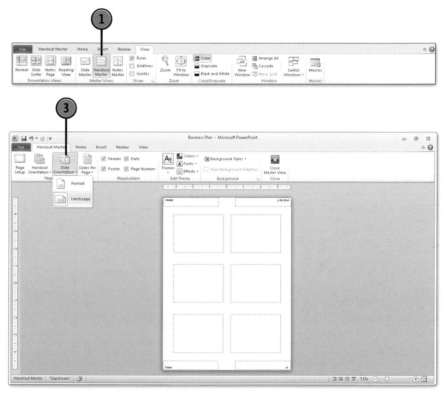

④ Click Slides Per Page, and choose an option from the gallery.

⑤ Click Background Styles, and choose a background for the handouts from the gallery.

⑥ Click the various tools in the Edit Theme group to choose formatting options from the various galleries.

⑦ Click Close Master View when you're done with handout master settings to return to Normal view.

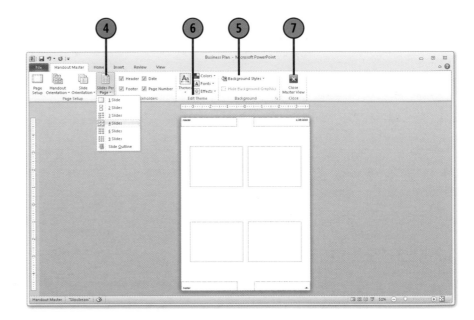

Try This!

You can use the Insert tab when in Handout Master view to insert graphics that appear only on your handouts. For example, you might want to insert a logo and the words "Company Confidential" on handouts to ensure that people treat the handouts as private.

Tip

To leave background graphics off handouts, which can make the text easier to read, select the Hide Background Graphics check box in the Background group on the Handout Master tab.

Work with Notes Master

① On the View tab, click Notes Master in the Master Views group.

② Click in a placeholder and enter text or replace the date or slide number element already there.

③ Drag a placeholder to a new location.

④ Clear check boxes to remove any of the six placeholders from handouts.

⑤ Click Slide Orientation or Notes Page Orientation, and choose Portrait or Landscape.

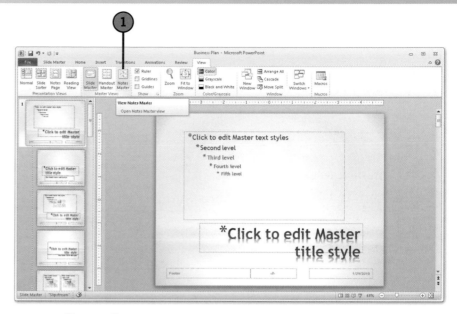

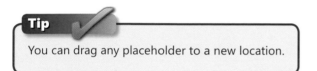

Tip

You can drag any placeholder to a new location.

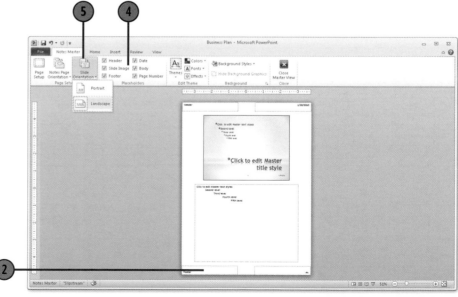

6 Click to choose a background for the handouts from the Background Styles gallery.

7 Click the tools in the Edit Theme group to choose formatting options from the various galleries.

8 Click Close Master View when you're done with notes master settings to return to Normal view.

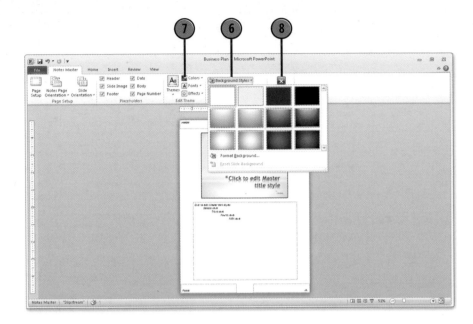

Tip

Be sure to format the notes body so that you can easily read your notes while making a presentation—often in a darkened room. Make the font size large, and use a font that is clean and easy to read.

See Also

For more information about formatting text to make it easily readable, see "Formatting Text" on page 145.

6

Building a Presentation

Although a presentation can contain text, graphics, animations, and special elements such as charts and WordArt, most presentations begin with you entering some kind of text. Text is used for the major headings for each slide as well as for the individual bullet points that provide the details of your topic. You can enter text in an outline or in placeholders on individual slides in Normal view in Microsoft PowerPoint 2010. (For more about entering text in an outline, see Section 7, "Building a Presentation Outline," starting on page 81.)

In this section you discover how to insert a new slide in your presentation and enter text on it. Once you enter text, you often need to edit it by modifying what you entered, cutting or copying text and then pasting it in new locations, or finding and replacing text. As you insert and edit text, knowing how to undo and redo actions as you go is another useful skill you'll be very glad to have, and it's covered in this section, too.

Finally, in this section you work with manipulating the placeholders where you enter text. You can apply formatting to placeholders and align the text within them. One other feature you learn about is the Selection And Visibility pane, which aides you in selecting and manipulating placeholders on slides.

Understanding How to Build a Presentation

You enter most text, as well as elements such as pictures and tables, by using placeholders on slides in Normal view. You can format placeholders to use fill colors and borders. Slide title and subtitle placeholders typically hold a single heading, while content placeholders are used to enter a bulleted list of key points. When you enter text in placeholders, it is reflected in the Outline tab in Normal view.

New Slide button

Outline created when you enter text

Slide title placeholder (main topic)

Placeholder with centered text

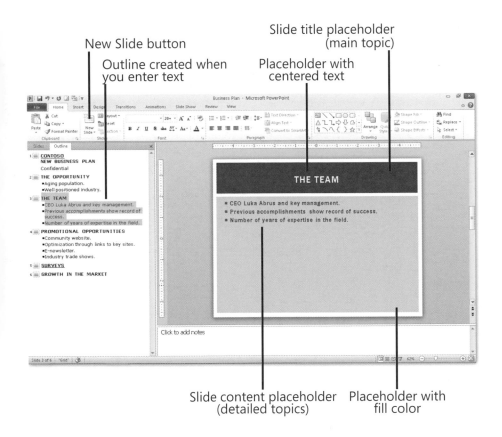

Slide content placeholder (detailed topics)

Placeholder with fill color

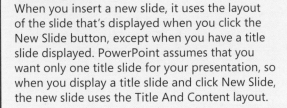

Try This!

There are other text-only slide layouts as well as a blank slide. Try inserting a Section Header or a Two Content slide layout from the Layout gallery. You can add text to a blank slide by using a text box (see "Add a Text Box" on page 141), but remember that text in a text box is not reflected in the presentation outline.

See Also

Although this section deals with the basics of inserting slides with a few different layouts, I deal with different slide layouts in more detail in Section 9, "Using Slide Layouts and Themes," starting on page 103.

Tip

When you insert a new slide, it uses the layout of the slide that's displayed when you click the New Slide button, except when you have a title slide displayed. PowerPoint assumes that you want only one title slide for your presentation, so when you display a title slide and click New Slide, the new slide uses the Title And Content layout.

Building a Slide

When you open a blank presentation, PowerPoint provides you with one blank title slide. A title slide contains two placeholders—a title and a subtitle. When you insert another slide, a slide that uses the Title And Content layout is inserted by default. This layout contains a title placeholder where you enter the topic for the slide and a placeholder for inserting bulleted points for that topic. Other slide layouts also use text placeholders, but these are the two types of slides you use most often for building presentation contents. (See Section 10, "Inserting Media and Drawing Objects," starting on page 113, for information about working with slide layouts that include graphic elements.)

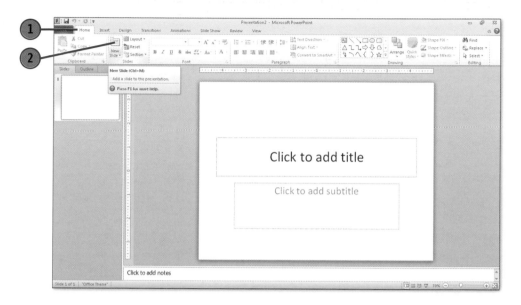

Insert a New Slide

① Click the Home tab.

② Click New Slide to insert a new title and content slide.

③ Click the arrow on the New Slide button, and then choose a layout option from the Office Theme gallery that appears. With this method, you can choose any layout you want as you're creating the new slide.

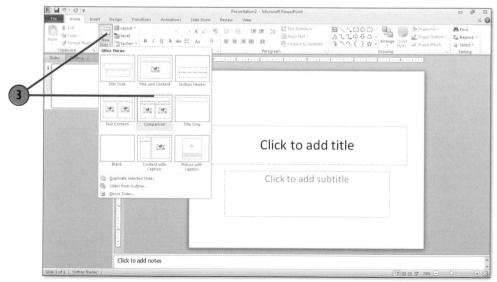

Enter Text on Slides

1 Click a title placeholder.

2 Type your text, and then click any-where outside the placeholder.

3 Click a content placeholder, and type one line of text, press Enter, and then type the next line of text. Bullet points are added automatically.

Tip

You can modify bullet point styles that are inserted in content placeholders. Click the arrow on the Bullets button in the Paragraph group on the Home tab and choose a different style, or click Bullets And Numbering at the bottom of the list to customize bullet styles.

See Also

For information about formatting text you type into placeholders, see "Formatting Text" on page 145.

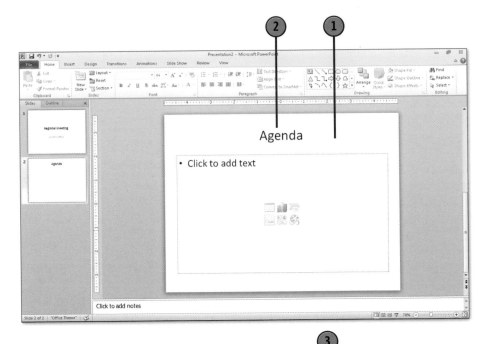

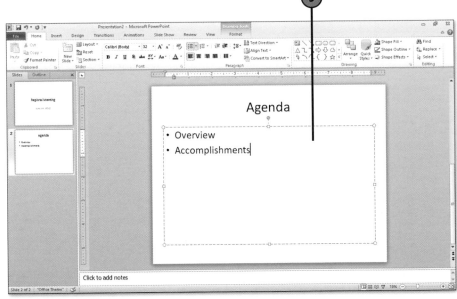

Insert a Symbol

① Click in a placeholder where you want to insert a symbol.

② Click the Insert tab.

③ Click Symbol.

④ Click the arrow on the Font list to choose a font set.

⑤ Scroll to locate the symbol you want to insert, and click it.

⑥ Click Insert. The symbol is inserted on the slide.

⑦ Continue to locate and insert symbols you need, and click Close when you're done.

Tip

All fonts have some symbols, such as percent and dollar signs, but if you're looking for little pictures or design elements rather than text, your best bet is to choose from these font sets: Symbol, Wingdings, Wingdings 2 or 3, or Webdings.

Try This!

For some font sets you can narrow down the symbols available in the Symbols dialog box by choosing a category from the Subset list. For example, if you want symbols only for international currencies, choose the Currency Symbols category, and if you want only arrow symbols, choose Arrows.

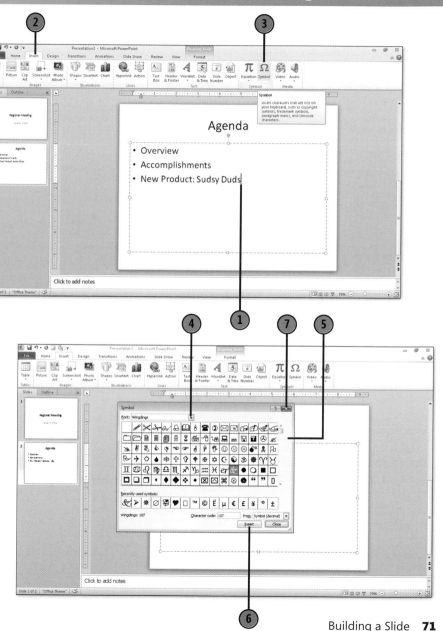

Insert the Date and Time

1. Click the placeholder where you want to insert the date and time.

2. Click the Insert tab.

3. Click Date & Time.

4. Click a date and time format.

5. Click OK.

Try This!

If you want the date and time to update whenever you print or show your presentation, select the Update Automatically check box in the Date And Time dialog box before you click OK in step 5.

Tip

You can also place the date and time in a footer on a slide master so that it appears on every slide in your presentation. See Section 5, "Working with Slide Masters," starting on page 53, for more about working with masters.

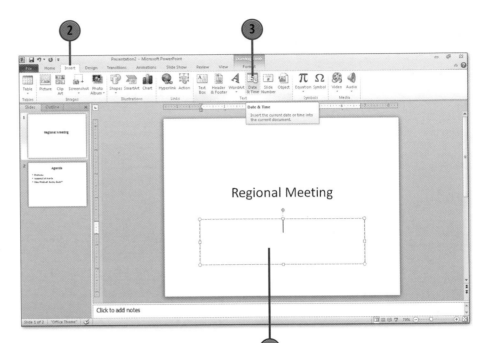

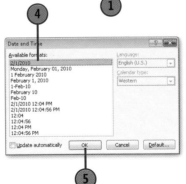

Working with Text

Most of us aren't letter perfect the first time we write something. We need to go back and make changes and even undo some things we've done. Sometimes we need to move some text from one spot to another. To help out with these tasks, PowerPoint makes it easy to shift things around when you change your mind. You can edit text; cut, copy, and paste text; and undo or redo actions.

Edit Text

1. Click in a placeholder at the location in the text that you want to edit. (If you select text to edit it, the Mini toolbar containing formatting tools appears.)

2. Take any of the following actions:

   - Press Delete to delete text to the right of the cursor one character at a time.

   - Press Backspace to delete text to the left of the cursor one character at a time.

   - Drag over text, and then press the Delete key to delete all selected text.

   - Begin typing any additional or replacement text.

3. Click outside the placeholder.

Tip

The Paste Special command allows you to paste text or objects that you cut or copy to your PowerPoint presentation in different formats, such as HTML, which is readable by Web browsers, or OLE (object linking and embedding), which pastes an icon rather than the actual content in your presentation. For more about working with a presentation outline, see Section 7.

See Also

For information about cutting, copying, and pasting entire slides or duplicating slide contents, see "Managing Slides in Slide Sorter View" on page 93.

Tip

You can also edit text in the Outline pane. Remember that any change you make to placeholder text on a slide is reflected in the outline and vice versa. See Section 7 for more about working with a presentation outline.

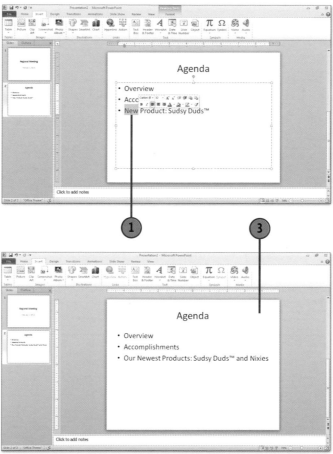

Undo and Redo an Action

(1) After performing an action such as typing, formatting, or moving an object, click the Undo [Action] button on the Quick Access Toolbar. The action is reversed.

(2) To redo an undone action, click the Redo [Action] button.

(3) If you want to undo a series of actions, click the arrow on the Undo [Action] button, and choose the actions from the list that appears.

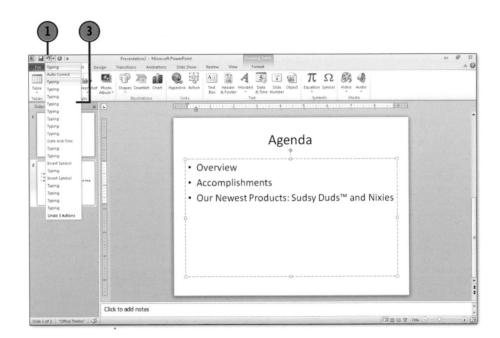

Tip

A quick and easy way to undo what you just did is to press Ctrl+Z. You can redo what you've undone by pressing Ctrl+Y.

Cut, Copy, and Paste Text

1 Click the Home tab.

2 Click the placeholder you want to copy, or drag to select text if you want to copy or cut and paste the text only (and not the placeholder).

3 Click Cut or Copy.

4 Click where you want to paste the cut or copied text.

5 Click Paste.

Tip

If you click the arrow on the Paste button you can choose from a variety of special paste options that might allow you to keep original formatting, use destination formatting, or paste in a special format.

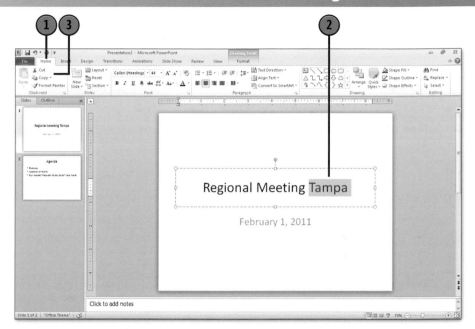

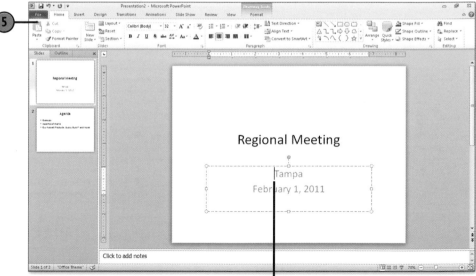

Finding and Replacing Text

Often when you create a presentation, you need to change every instance of a word or phrase. For example, your company might change the name of a product under development. In that case, finding and editing each instance manually can be time-consuming. Use the Find and Replace feature to easily find every instance and change them all instantly or one by one.

Find and Replace Text

① Click the Home tab.

② Click Find.

③ Enter a word or phrase you want to find and change.

④ Click Replace.

⑤ Enter the word or phrase with which you want to replace the original text.

⑥ Do one of the following:

- Click Find Next to find the next instance of the text.

- Click Replace to replace the currently selected instance of the text.

- Click Replace All to replace all instances of the text. Note that you are not asked to confirm this choice, but you can use the Undo action to revert changes if anything disastrous happens!

⑦ When you finish finding or replacing text, PowerPoint displays a confirming message. Click OK.

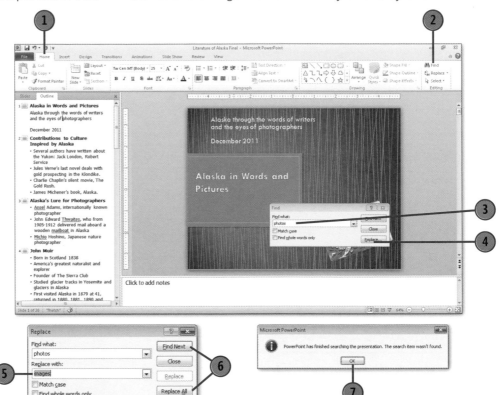

Tip

Use the Match Case and Find Whole Words Only check boxes in the Find And Replace dialog box to narrow your search. If, for instance, you want to find the word Bell (a last name) and you don't want lowercase instances of the word bell or words such as bellow, you could use both of these qualifiers in your find and replace operation.

Manipulating Placeholders

With the exception of text boxes (covered in Section 10), place-holders are where you create the elements of your presentation. They contain text, drawings, pictures, charts, and more. Placeholders provide an easy way to arrange the components of each slide, and because they come with certain predesigned formatting, they make adding everything from a bulleted list to a chart easy. By selecting a placeholder (made easier with the Selection And Visibility pane), you can align the contents of placeholders and format their backgrounds and borders.

Use the Selection And Visibility Pane

1. Display the slide you want to work on in Normal view, and click the Home tab.

2. Click Select in the Editing group, and choose Selection Pane.

Tip

In addition to using the Selection And Visibility pane to help you select objects, you can click the Arrange button on the Home tab and use the Bring To Front and Send To Back buttons to move a selected item in a stack of items to the front or back of others.

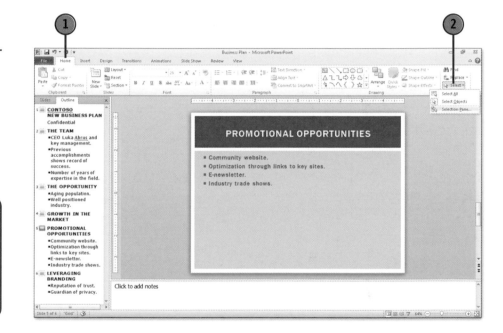

Visibility button

③ In the Selection And Visibility pane, do any of the following:

- Click an item in the Shapes On This Slide list to select the object.

- Click Hide All to hide all items.

- Click Show All for an item again to display the item.

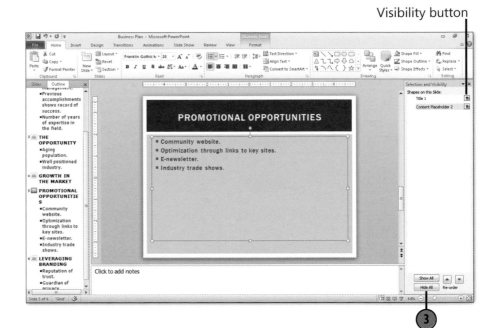

Tip

If you click an object, the Format tab appears on the ribbon. This tab also contains the Arrange group of tools, including the Selection Pane, Bring To Front, and Send To Back buttons.

See Also

For more information about working with objects on your slides, see Section 10.

Align Placeholder Contents

① Click the placeholder containing the text you want to align, and then click the Home tab.

② If you want to align only one line of several, select the text you want to align.

③ Click any of the alignment buttons, and the text shifts accordingly.

Caution

Themes that you apply to your slides provide a certain design balance to elements on the page. Be sure that if you shift the alignment of text in placeholders that the text is balanced on the slide against any graphics or master elements such as footers.

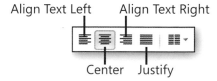

Align Text Left   Align Text Right

Center   Justify

Tip

Use centered text for emphasis for a single line of text. If you're working with bulleted lists, you should usually use left or justified alignment so that each bulleted item begins at the same place, making the list easier to follow.

Formatting Placeholders

1. Right-click the placeholder border, and choose Format Shape from the shortcut menu.

2. Click a category on the left.

3. Choose settings to add a fill color, add and adjust a border line, or add a shadow or 3-D effect. Notice that whatever settings you make are previewed on the placeholder.

4. Click Close to apply your new settings.

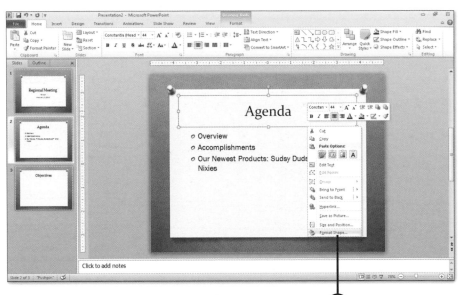

Caution

Don't go overboard adding effects to placeholders, especially if your slide contains a lot of graphics and text. Let the text be the important element on any slide to help get your message across.

Tip

After you apply a fill color to a placeholder, a quick way to change the fill color is to select the placeholder, click the Shape Fill button on the Format tab, and then choose a new color scheme for the presentation.

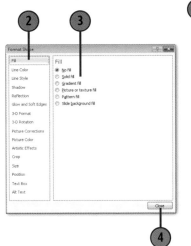

7

Building a Presentation Outline

A tool for organizing your thoughts and information that has been around for quite some time is the outline. An outline breaks down information into multiple headings and subheading levels.

The outlining feature in Microsoft PowerPoint 2010 helps you use this valuable tool to enter text, reorganize it into topics and subtopics, and reorder the contents of your presentation.

You access the outlining feature from the Outline tab in the Slides/Outline pane in Normal view. If you are focused on entering a lot of text and not as much on the look of individual slides, it can be faster to enter that text in the Outline tab rather than on each individual slide.

When you enter text on a slide, the content is reflected in the outline, and vice versa. As you work in the outline, the slide that corresponds to the text you're working on appears in the Slide pane, so you can see how changes to the outline affect the slide.

Another nice aspect of the outlining feature in PowerPoint is that you can cut and paste an outline you create in a Microsoft Word document into the Outline pane, where it can form the basis of your presentation. You can also copy text in the Outline pane of PowerPoint and paste it into a Word document to create a written report or a useful audience handout.

Understanding the Relationship of the Outline to Slides

Different slide layouts contain different placeholders, such as title, subtitle, text, and content placeholders. You can enter text in the placeholders on a slide or in the Outline tab of the Slides/Outline pane. When you enter text into title, subtitle, or text placeholders in the Slide pane, the text also appears in the outline. When you enter a top-level heading in the outline, PowerPoint creates a new slide, and that heading appears

in the slide title placeholder. Any text that you enter at an indented level in the Outline pane becomes a bullet point in a text placeholder on the slide.

Graphics do not appear in the outline. Text that you enter in text boxes (which are drawing objects that are different from text placeholders) also doesn't appear in the outline.

Outline View button
Outline tab
Slide pane

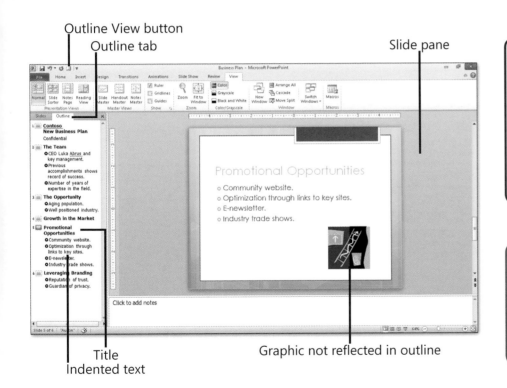

Title
Indented text

Graphic not reflected in outline

Tip

What if you want to see a thumbnail of a slide but need more room to work in the outline? You can expand the Outline tab so that it fills about three-quarters of the screen, which leaves you with a small preview of the slide in the Slide pane and large, easy-to-read outline contents. To expand the Outline tab, drag the divider between the Outline tab and the Slide pane to the right as far as you can.

Try This!

If you have a long presentation and you expand the Outline tab to view more of the outline, the slide preview may be too small to be readable. Drag the zoom slider at the bottom-right corner of the PowerPoint window to quickly enlarge the slide preview but not the outline text.

Working with the Outline

You can work on an outline in the Outline tab in the Slides/Outline pane displayed at the left of the Slide pane in Normal view. The Outline tab lets you compare the outline with slides, which might include graphics or text boxes that don't show up in the outline. Entering text in the outline can be faster than entering it on individual slides when you're focused purely on presentation text content.

Display the Outline Tab

① Click the View tab and then click the Normal View button.

② Click the Outline tab.

③ Click the Outline View button on the Quick Access Toolbar to display the Outline view. (You may have to add this button to the toolbar by using PowerPoint Options.)

See Also

You can format text in both the Outline tab and the Slide pane to change the size or type. A change made in one place is reflected in the other. For more about changing text format, see "Formatting Text" on page 145.

See Also

You can add the Slides From Outline button to the Quick Access Toolbar. See "Customizing the Quick Access Toolbar" on page 29. When you click the button, you can insert an outline created in a word processor as slides in a blank presentation.

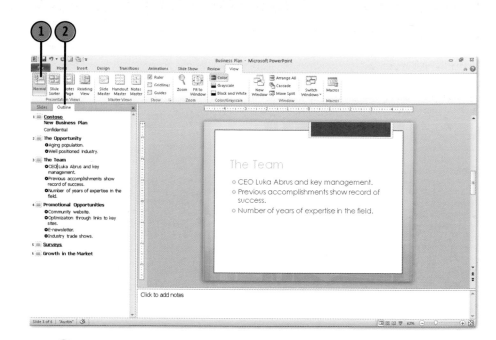

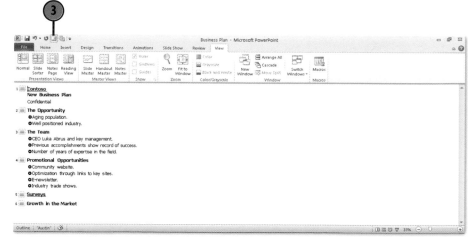

Adding Text in the Outline Tab

One of the benefits of the Outline tab is that it provides a fast way for you to enter text without having to deal with placeholders or graphics. After you enter the title, adding text to the outline consists of pressing Enter to create a new entry in the outline and then entering the text, which appears at the same outline level as the line before. You can then demote text to become a subheading (subtitle or bullet point) or promote a bullet point to become the next slide title.

Add a Slide Title

(1) With the Outline tab selected in Normal view, click in the outline.

(2) Enter some text, which is automatically formatted as a slide title, and press Enter. The slide title appears in both the outline and the Slide pane, and the cursor is in place to create the next slide title.

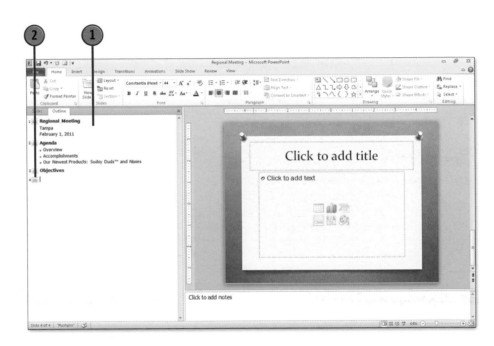

Tip

The first slide is always created using the Title Slide layout. There is typically only one title slide in a presentation, although you could duplicate it and place the duplicate at the end of your presentation. A title slide consists of a title and subtitle. After the first slide, other slides you insert use the layout of the slide that's selected when you insert them by default.

See Also

For more information about slide layouts, see "Understanding What Slide Layouts and Themes Control" on page 104.

Promote and Demote Headings

 Enter text in the Outline tab, or click in an existing line of text to select it.

 Click the Home tab, and choose Decrease List Level or Increase List Level from the Paragraph group. Decrease demotes the heading; Increase promotes it to a higher level in the outline.

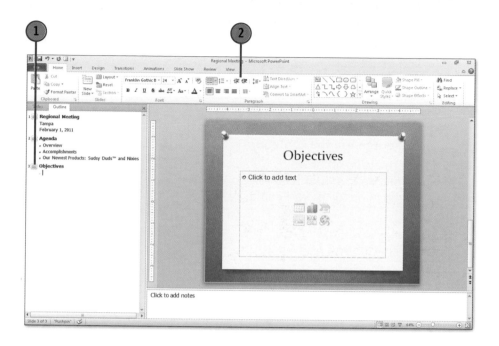

Tip

You can create many levels of indented bullets in an outline, but a couple of levels is usually the most you should ever have. As a rule, if you have that much detail to provide about a point, it really should be on a separate slide. Also, in the typical presentation environment, attendees can't possibly see more than two levels of headings on the screen.

Tip

After you demote a heading to the bullet point level, when you press Enter to create the next heading, that heading is also at the bullet point level. When you're ready to start the next slide, you can type a heading and then promote it to slide title level. You can also use a shortcut to do this: press Shift+Tab to promote a heading or Tab to demote it.

Try This!

In PowerPoint 2010, when you select text, a Mini toolbar containing the most commonly used text formatting tools appears. You can use the Promote and Demote buttons on the Mini toolbar to structure your outline.

Working with Outline Contents

Once you enter your contents in your outline and demote and promote headings to create an outline structure, you might want to work with the outline contents in various ways. For example, at times you might want to view just the slide titles; at other times, you want to see all the detailed headings. You might also want to move headings around in an outline to reorganize the content.

Finally, text formatting is shown by default in an outline, but you can turn it off and back on easily, which can come in handy as you edit and review your slides.

Expand and Collapse the Outline

1. Click the Outline tab to display it, and then right-click a slide.

2. Do either of the following to collapse the outline:
   - Choose Collapse to hide all the sub-heads for this slide title.
   - Choose Collapse All to hide all the subheads for the presentation.

3. Do either of the following to expand the outline:
   - Choose Expand to display all the subheads for this slide title.
   - Choose Expand All to display all subheads in the presentation.

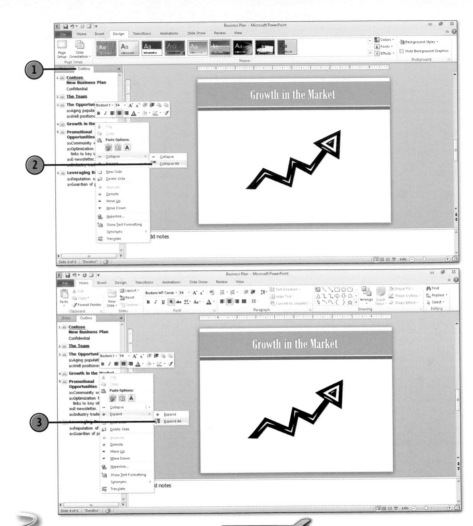

Try This!

In a longer presentation, collapse headings for slides that you've finished working on to speed up scrolling through your outline to find information you need. When you are ready to view all your contents again, right-click in the Outline tab and choose Expand, Expand All.

Tip

Collapsing or expanding your outline has no effect on what appears in the Slide pane or on what appears when you give your slide presentation. A presentation in which you have collapsed the outline still shows all headings at every level when you display Slide Show view.

Move Slides or Text Up and Down in an Outline

1. Right-click the line of text or right-click and drag to select multiple lines of text that you want to move.

2. Choose Move Up or Move Down from the shortcut menu. The selected line or lines move one line up or down together.

3. To move an entire slide, you can drag the slide icon to a new position in the outline. A line appears, indicating the position of the text as you drag.

See Also

For information about editing text in slides, see "Edit Text" on page 73.

Tip

If slide subheads are collapsed under the title and you move the title, all subheads move along with their slide title. If you don't want to move a subhead, you must first expand the slide and either move the subhead to another family of headings (by cutting and pasting it elsewhere) or promote it to be a slide title on its own.

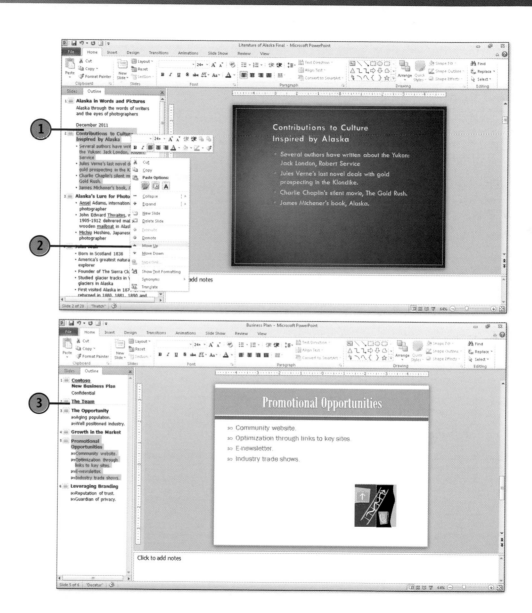

Turn Formatting On and Off in an Outline

1 Right-click anywhere in the Outline tab.

2 Choose Show Text Formatting from the shortcut menu.

3 To return text to the way it was, right-click in the Outline tab and choose Show Text Formatting again.

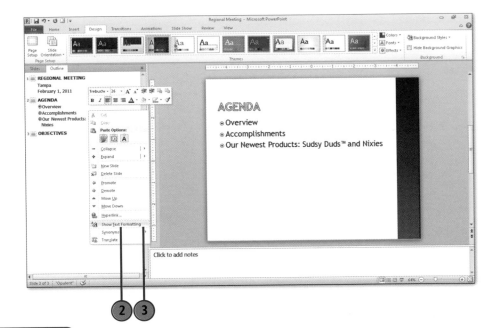

Tip

Showing formatting in the outline is a good way to see whether you have a balance of fonts or formats such as bold in your presentation and to confirm that you have kept text formatting consistent overall. Another good way to view this is to display Slide Sorter view.

Insert a Word Outline into PowerPoint

1. Choose New from the File menu; click Blank Presentation and then click the Create button.

2. If necessary, add the Slides From Outline button to the Quick Access Toolbar (click the Customize Quick Access Toolbar button, choose More Commands, click Slides From Outline, click Add, and then click OK) and then click it.

3. In the Insert Outline dialog box, locate the Word document you want to use, and click Open. The outline content appears as slides in the blank presentation.

Tip

You can also cut text from the PowerPoint Outline pane and paste it into Word to create a Word outline from it.

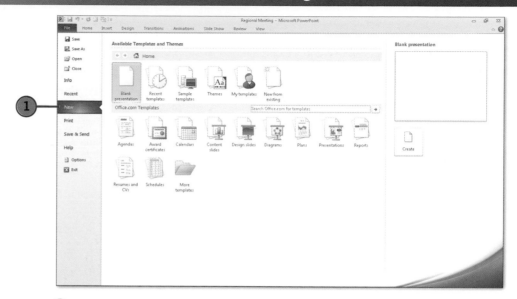

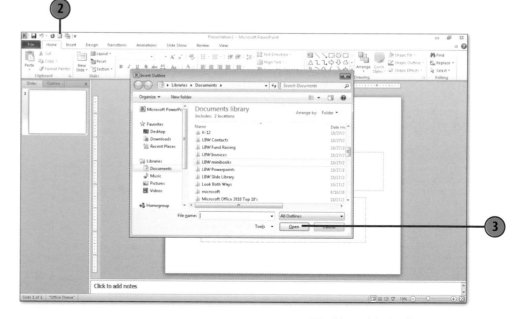

8

Managing and Viewing Slides

Once you create some slides, you often need to work with them to refine your content. For example, you might want to move among your slides to review their content, delete or copy certain slides, move slides, or hide them in the presentation.

The Slides tab is useful for viewing the slides in your presentation as thumbnails, which appear next to the larger view of the selected slide displayed in Normal view.

Sometimes while refining a presentation, you need to delete a slide that's no longer relevant or copy and paste a slide from one place—or presentation—into another. Microsoft PowerPoint 2010 also has a handy, one-step feature to duplicate a slide by copying and pasting. If the content of your presentation needs reorganizing, you can move slides around quite easily in Slide Sorter view.

You can use the new Section feature to break up larger presentations so that you can focus on the portion you want to work on. Sections are displayed both on the Slides tab in Normal view and in Slide Sorter view.

Finally, you can choose not to show certain slides while running your presentation by hiding them. You can easily unhide them when you need to use them again. Hiding and unhiding slides makes it easy to customize presentations for different audiences.

Viewing Slides in the Slide Pane

PowerPoint offers several views of your slides. In Normal view, the Slide pane is the central display area for the currently selected slide. Typically, this is where you focus on the design elements of each slide. In addition, the Slides tab, which is cou- pled with the Outline tab to the left of the Slide pane, shows all the slides in your presentation in order. Use this tab to see an overview of the look and contents of all slides side by side, with one slide shown in more detail.

Display Slides

① Click the Slides tab in the Slides/Outline pane in Normal view. The Slides tab appears.

② From the Slides tab, do any of the follow- ing to move around in your presentation:

- Click the Scroll Down button to move ahead in the presentation.

- Click the Scroll Up button to move back in the presentation.

- Drag the scroll bar to move ahead or back in the presentation by one or more slides at a time.

- Click just above or just below the scroll bar to move ahead or back in the pres- entation by one slide at a time.

③ Click a slide to select it. The slide is then displayed in the Slide pane.

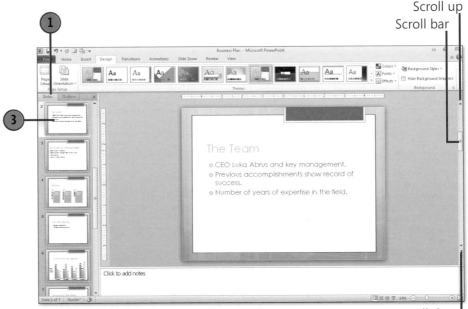

Scroll up

Scroll bar

Scroll down

 Tip

Can't find the Slides tab? If the Slides/Outline pane is not vis- ible in Normal view, you closed it at some point. Just click the Normal View button to restore it.

Try This!

You can resize the Slides tab to see more or fewer of the slides in your presentation and to enlarge the contents of each slide. Click the border between the Slides tab and the Slide pane and drag it to the right to enlarge the Slides tab (it can't be expanded larger than a few inches) and to the left to shrink it.

Managing Slides in Slide Sorter View

As with anything you write, part of the process of building a PowerPoint presentation is revising and refining your content as you go along. Just as you edit a report by deleting or copying a sentence, you might delete a slide in a PowerPoint presentation or copy a slide so that you can base a new slide on existing content. It's also typical to rearrange the flow of your thoughts as you write. In PowerPoint, that's as easy as moving a slide around in your presentation. All these tasks are simple to do in Slide Sorter view.

Delete Slides

① Click the Slide Sorter View button to display Slide Sorter view.

② Right-click a slide.

③ Choose Delete Slide from the shortcut menu.

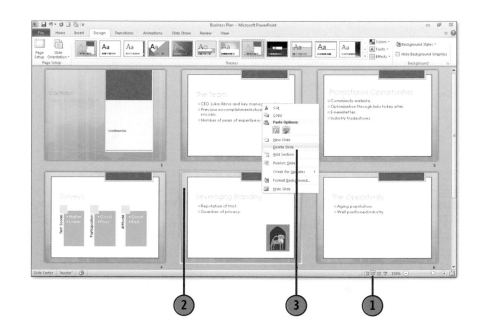

Tip

You can use the Zoom slider in the bottom-right corner of the PowerPoint window to zoom in on and out of the selected slide's contents in the Slide pane. If you zoom out and enlarge the contents and then need more space to show the enlarged slide on your screen, you can shrink the Slides tab by using the method described in the Try This tip on the previous page.

Caution

If you delete a slide and exit PowerPoint, that slide is gone forever. Be sure you don't need any of a slide's contents before you delete it.

See Also

Instead of deleting a slide, you can temporarily hide it from view. Then, if you decide you need the contents later, you can simply unhide it. See "Hiding and Unhiding Slides" on page 97 for help with this feature.

Copy and Paste Slides

1. With Slide Sorter view displayed, click a slide.

2. Click the Home tab on the ribbon.

3. Click the Copy button.

4. Click the slide you want to paste the original slide after.

5. On the Home tab, click Paste.

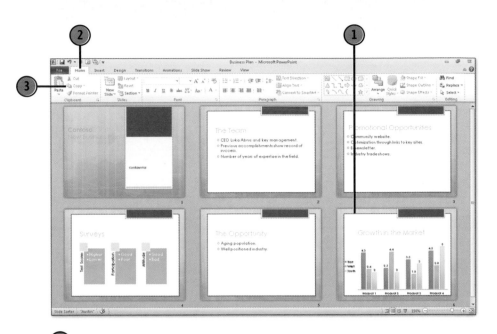

Tip

You can also use keyboard shortcuts to cut, copy, and paste selected slides. Keyboard shortcuts are displayed in the Enhanced ScreenTip that appears when you hold your mouse over an item on the ribbon. Use Ctrl+X to cut, Ctrl+C to copy, and Ctrl+V to paste.

See Also

Use the procedures here to cut, copy, and paste whole slides. For more about cutting, copying, and pasting specific elements from the contents of slides, see "Cut, Copy, and Paste Text" on page 75.

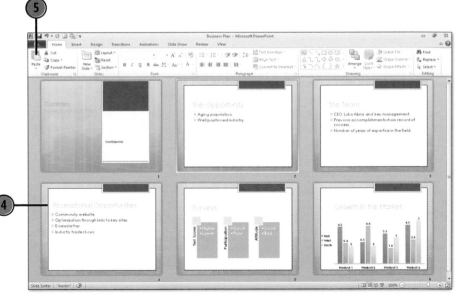

Duplicate Slides

 With Slide Sorter view displayed, click a slide.

 On the ribbon, click the Home tab.

③ Click the arrow on the New Slide button, and choose Duplicate Selected Slides. The duplicate slide appears to the right of the original slide.

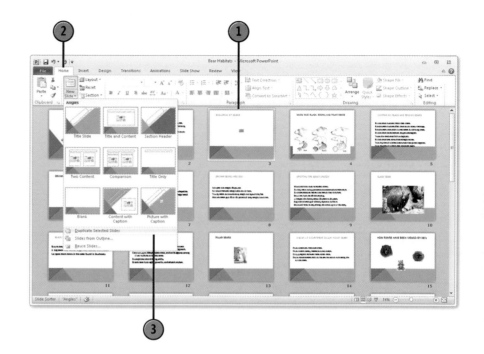

Tip

After you duplicate a slide, you can move the duplicate wherever you want in the presentation and make changes to it. See the next task for more about moving slides.

Tip

You can also cut, copy, paste, and duplicate slides by using the Slides tab in Normal view. Just right-click any slide on the tab, and choose the appropriate command from the shortcut menu that appears.

Move a Slide

1 With Slide Sorter view displayed, click a slide.

2 Drag the slide to where you want it to appear in the presentation. A vertical line indicates the new position.

3 Release the mouse button to place the slide in the new position.

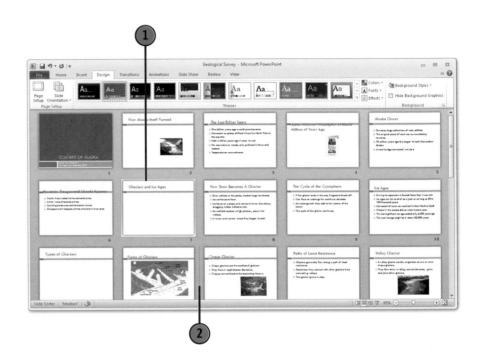

Tip

You can use the Outline tab in Normal view to move slides around in text form. Right-click a slide icon and choose Move Up or Move Down to move a slide one position at a time, or drag the slide icon to any other position in the outline.

See Also

For more about managing slides in the Outline tab, see "Move Slides or Text Up and Down in an Outline" on page 87.

Hiding and Unhiding Slides

Sometimes you might want to use a subset of slides for a presentation, or perhaps you need to hide a single slide because it contains information not appropriate for a particular audience. For example, you might choose not to show a management benefits slide when you're making a presentation about benefits to nonmanagers. In that case, you can easily hide the slide, give the presentation, and then unhide it.

Hide Slides

(1) Click the Slide Sorter View button.

(2) Click a slide to select it. If you want to hide more than one contiguous slide, click the first slide, hold down Shift, and then click the last slide. To select noncontiguous slides, click the first one, hold down Ctrl, and then click additional slides to select them.

(3) On the ribbon, click the Slide Show tab.

(4) In the Set Up group, click Hide Slide to hide all selected slides. A gray box appears over the slide number, indicating that it is hidden; the slide does not appear when you run the presentation.

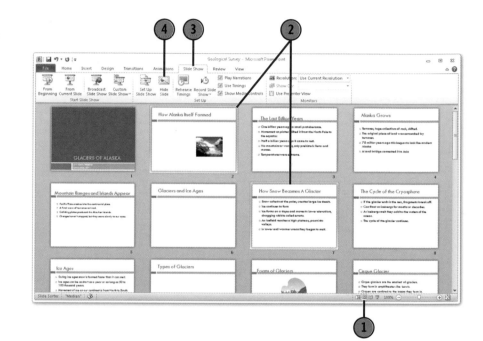

Unhide Slides

(1) With Slide Sorter view displayed, click the slide or slides you want to unhide.

(2) On the Slide Show tab, click Hide Slide in the Set Up group. The gray box disappears from around the slide number. The slide now appears when you run the presentation.

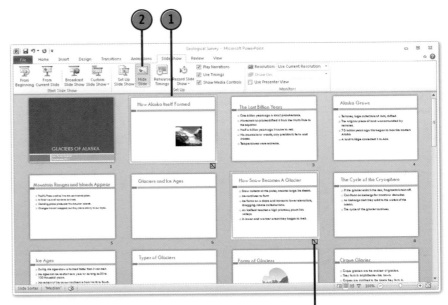

Hidden slide icon

Try This!

Try printing a presentation that includes hidden slides. When you display the Print options on the File tab in Backstage view, you can click the Print Hidden Slides check box in the Print pane so that slides you've hidden are included in the printout.

See Also

For more information about printing presentations with hidden slides, see "Choose Which Slides to Print" on page 214.

Working with Sections

Sections are a new feature in PowerPoint 2010 that help you find your way around larger presentations more easily. They function something like headings in a long report, helping you find groups of slides that address similar topics. When you create a section and name it, its name appears in a bar separating the slides within the section from others in the presentation. You can use a feature on that bar to expand or collapse sections, which is useful for focusing on just one section at a time.

Add a Section

1. Click the Slide Sorter View button.

2. Click to the left of the first slide in the next section.

3. On the Home tab, click Section, and then choose Add Section.

4. Repeat steps 1 through 3 to create additional sections.

Try This!

Create several sections in your presentation, and then in Slide Sorter view, click the small arrow to the left of a section's name to collapse it. Click the arrow again to expand that section. Experiment with using this feature to more easily navigate through a larger presentation.

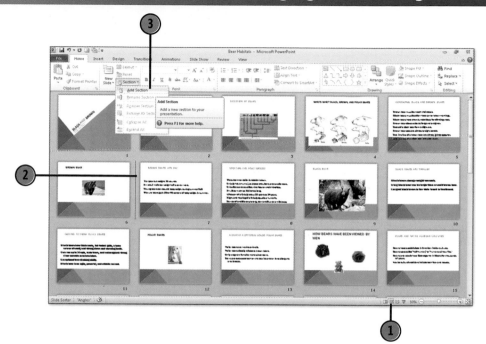

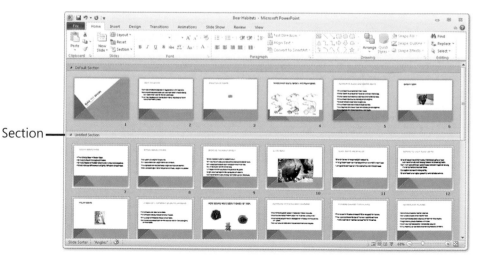

Section

Rename a Section

① Click the Slide Sorter View button.

② Right-click a section.

③ Choose Rename Section from the shortcut menu.

④ In the Rename Section dialog box, enter a new name and click Rename.

Tip

You can also work with sections from the Slides tab in Normal view. Right-click the section to work with the same shortcut menu displayed in step 3 above.

Try This!

You can also rearrange sections in your presentation by choosing Move Section Up or Move Section Down from the shortcut menu that appears when you right-click a section.

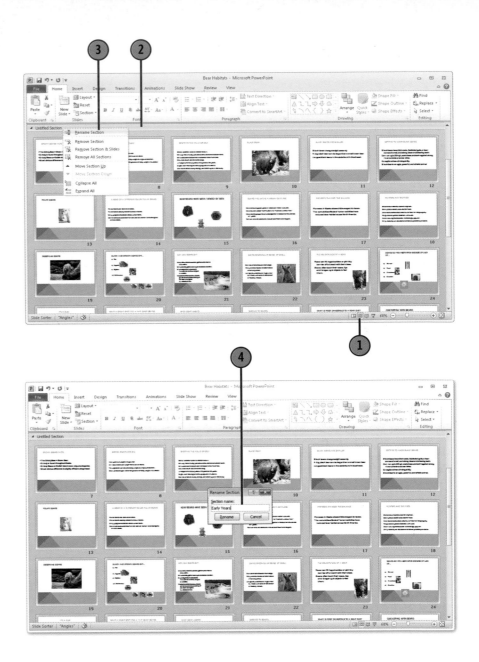

Delete a Section

① Click the Slide Sorter View button.

② Right-click a slide and choose Remove Section from the shortcut menu. The section (but not the slides within it) disappears.

Tip ✓

If you want to get rid of all your sections at some point, choose Remove All Sections from the shortcut menu that appears when you right-click a section. If you want to get rid of both a section and the slides within it, choose Remove Section & Slides.

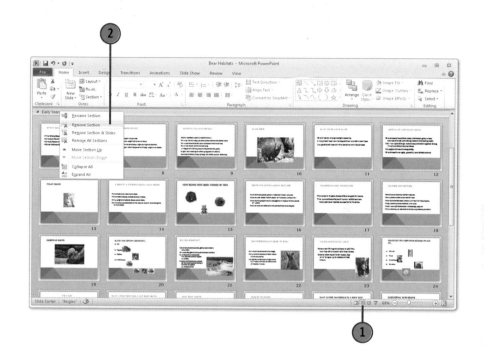

Using Slide Layouts and Themes

A presentation has to have solid content and clearly fleshed-out topics, but it must also hold your audience's attention. Visual enhancements such as color, font styles, and graphics go a long way toward impressing your audience with your professional approach.

Microsoft has built in several design aspects for your presentations in PowerPoint 2010. These design elements, including themes, color schemes, and slide layouts, offer a built-in consistency through a common look and feel. This design consistency means that you don't have to be a graphic designer to design an attractive presentation.

Themes can be applied to individual slides or to multiple slides in your presentation. A theme includes background colors, graphics, font styles and sizes, and alignment of placeholders and text.

Layouts control how many and what types of placeholders appear on a slide. For example, a layout might contain only a slide title placeholder or a slide title plus content placeholders. (Content placeholders can contain several kinds of content, such as a chart, table, picture, SmartArt object, or video.)

Color schemes are preset combinations of colors for your slide backgrounds, text, and graphic elements.

Understanding What Slide Layouts and Themes Control

Slide layouts provide a basic structure to your slides by including placeholders that can contain title or subtitle text, bulleted lists, or a variety of graphic elements (referred to as content) in a variety of combinations. By selecting the right slide layout, you make the job of adding text and content easier because placeholders can help to automate the building of slides.

While slide layouts control the types of slide content, slide themes are concerned with the design elements of a slide. These might include a background color or an effect such as a gradient; font styles, sizes, and alignment; bullet styles; and graphic elements.

Layout gallery

Slide title placeholder with text (main topic)

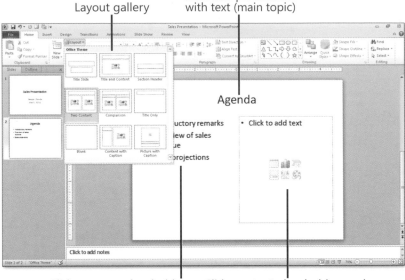

Slide content placeholder containing text

Slide content placeholder ready for text or graphic content

Font

Theme gallery

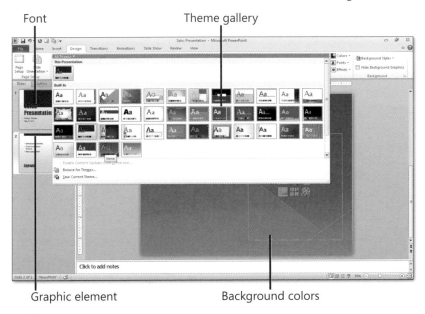

Graphic element

Background colors

Working with Layouts

A slide layout in PowerPoint is like a blueprint for a house; it establishes the various types of "rooms" that appear on your slide. Just as certain types of rooms contain certain types of furniture, slides can contain different types of objects. A title and content slide holds a title and bullet list, while a picture with caption layout can hold an image and text describing it.

Apply a Layout

(1) Display the slide whose layout you want to change, and click the Home tab.

(2) Click Layout to open the Layout gallery.

(3) Click a layout to apply it.

You can determine a slide's layout when you first create it. Click the Home tab, and then click the arrow on the New Slide button. Click the layout you prefer, and the slide is created with that layout applied.

Tip

PowerPoint 2003 and earlier versions include slide layouts with bullet point content and others with graphic and multimedia content. In PowerPoint 2010 and 2007, layouts with content now include both bullet point and graphic/multimedia content tools on one slide. You have to pick one or the other, though: when you use either of these tools to add content to these placeholders, the other tool disappears.

The placeholders in a layout automate tasks involved with creating and formatting content specific to each type of placeholder.

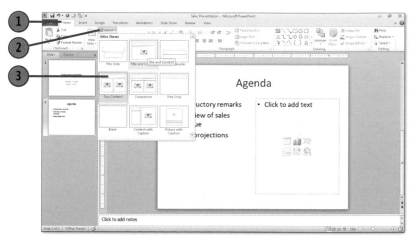

The number of placeholders specified by that layout appears

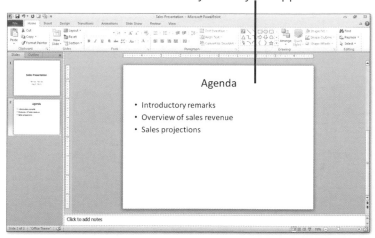

Add a Placeholder to a Slide Layout

① Click the View tab.

② Click Slide Master. The slide master appears.

③ Click Insert Placeholder.

④ Select a style of placeholder to insert.

Tip

If you'd rather create an additional placeholder on only one slide, try duplicating an existing placeholder. First, select the placeholder on the slide. Then, on the Home tab, click the arrow on the Copy button and choose the Duplicate command. A copy of the placeholder is pasted on the slide.

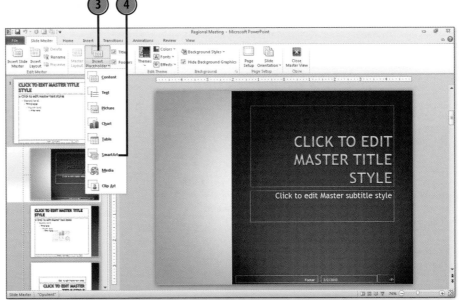

⑤ Click the slide, and then drag to draw the placeholder where you want it to appear.

⑥ If necessary, click the placeholder to select it, and then drag it to a new position on the slide.

⑦ Click the Close Master View button to close the slide master. The additional placeholder now appears on every slide of that type in the presentation.

See Also

For information about working in Slide Master view, see "Making Changes to a Slide Master" on page 55.

Working with Themes

Themes in PowerPoint provide a suite of design settings that give your slides a consistent look and feel. You can apply a theme with a single action, putting in place background graph-ics and colors and font and font size settings. The gallery of themes located on the Design tab helps you preview and easily choose the best look for your presentation.

Apply a Slide Theme

① Click the Design tab.

② Click the More arrow in the Themes gallery.

Tip

You can find additional themes online. Because nearly everybody who creates PowerPoint pres-entations picks from the same set of built-in themes, at some point you may want to show folks something entirely new. Finding updated themes becomes a way to differentiate your presentation.

See Also

For information about making individual changes to design elements on slides, see Section 11, "Formatting Text, Objects, and Slides," starting on page 143.

(3) Move your mouse pointer over the themes to preview them on your slides.

(4) Right-click a theme, and then click one of two options:

- Choose Apply To All Slides to apply the theme to every slide in your presentation.

- Choose Apply To Selected Slides to apply the theme only to the currently selected slide or slides.

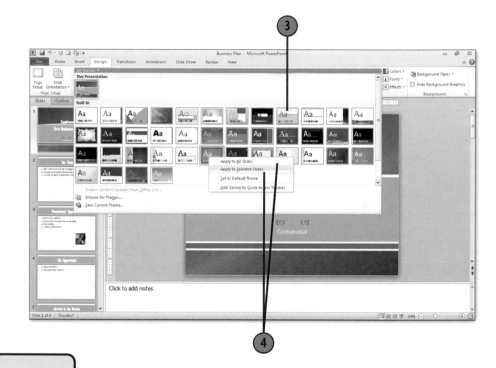

See Also

When you apply a new theme, it creates a master. For more information about working with slide masters, see "Understanding How Slide Masters Work" on page 54.

Tip

If you want to apply a theme to several slides, it's easiest to display Slide Sorter view, click the first slide you want to apply the theme to, and then hold down the Ctrl key and click other slides. Follow the preceding steps to apply the theme to the selected slides.

Find Slide Themes Online

① With your computer logged on to the Internet, click the File tab.

② Click New.

③ Enter a search term in the Search Office.com For Templates search box.

④ Click the Start Searching button.

⑤ In the results that appear, click a thumbnail.

Tip

By default, the blank Office theme is applied to new presentations. You can set a different theme as the default theme to be applied to every new presentation. First locate the theme in the Theme gallery, and then right-click it and select Set As Default Theme.

---

⑥ Click the Download button to download the template. PowerPoint automatically opens a new presentation with your new template applied.

Tip

If you can't find a theme you thought you downloaded, try choosing the Browse For Themes command at the bottom of the Theme gallery. In the Choose Theme Or Themed Document dialog box, enter the name of the theme (the Office Themes and Themed Document format is specified by default) or use tools to browse for the theme in the various folders on your computer.

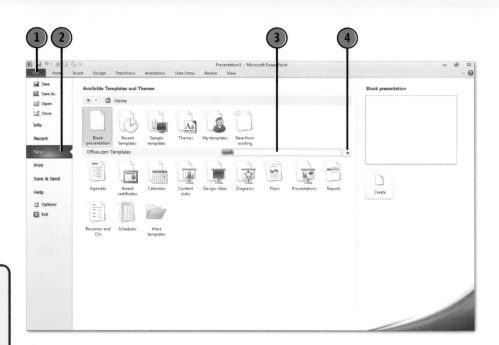

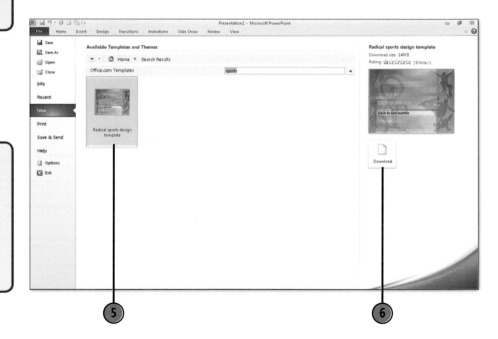

Changing Theme Colors and Fonts

Themes include settings for colors and fonts. A theme's color scheme affects most elements on your slide, including background, text, and graphics. Themes provide sets of colors that work well together, so your slides maintain an attractive and cohesive look. Font schemes include settings for heading and body fonts. When you apply a theme, it contains a preset color scheme and fonts, but you can change these to give your slides a different look.

Select a Different Theme Color Scheme

① Click the Design tab.

② Click Colors in the Themes group.

③ Right-click a color scheme, and choose Apply To All Slides or Apply To Selected Slides.

Tip ✓

Be sure to use color combinations that work well in the space where you will give your presentation. Most color combinations PowerPoint offers should help to keep your text readable, but if you decide to change the color of an individual element yourself, remember that light text colors are hard to read in a lighter space.

See Also

You can also apply theme elements to all slides by applying them through the slide master. For more information about working with masters, see "Display and Navigate Masters" on page 55.

Change Theme Fonts

1 Click the Design tab.

2 Click Fonts.

3 Move your mouse pointer over the fonts to preview them on your slides.

4 Click a font style to apply it to all slides.

Try This!

To create your own font theme, choose Create New Theme Fonts from the Fonts gallery. Select a heading font and body font, give the font theme a name, and click Save. The theme is now available in the Fonts gallery.

See Also

To learn how to manually change fonts for selected text, see "Applying Fonts" on page 144.

10

Inserting Media and Drawing Objects

The ability to add graphical elements to your slides lets you add a visual pizzazz to your presentation that helps keep viewers entertained and interested. In a multimedia-savvy world, people expect more than black bullet points and a white background, and Microsoft PowerPoint 2010 helps you meet those expectations.

Although visual elements should never overpower the message of your presentation, some visual elements, such as photographs or charts, might actually help you convey your message in a "picture is worth a thousand words" way. Sometimes you use elements such as illustrations, shapes, or WordArt effects simply to add visual interest. Using video or audio clips allows you to bring other people into the presentation to make a point or give a testimonial or demonstrate a product feature.

In this section, you explore the process of inserting various visual elements into slides—tables, charts, pictures, clip art, WordArt, audio, and even video clips. Once you insert such elements, move on to Section 11, "Formatting Text, Objects, and Slides," starting on page 143, where you discover how to format and modify those elements to best effect.

Working with Tables

Tables allow you to arrange information in cells organized by rows and columns to show the relationships among various sets of data. Tables offer the option of formatting those columns and rows with color and shading, which helps the person viewing the table differentiate the sets of data at a glance.

Insert a Table

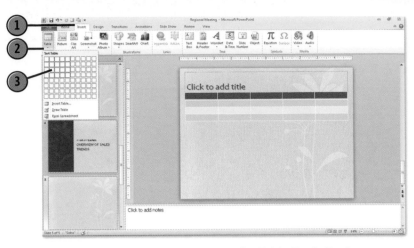

1. Click the Insert tab.

2. Click Table.

3. In the Insert Table drop-down, drag across the squares to select the number of rows and columns you want to include in your table.

4. Release your mouse.

Try This!

You can also insert a table by using an icon in the set of icons that appears in any empty content placeholder. Click the icon at the upper left to display a dialog box where you can specify the number of rows and columns for the table.

Try This!

The Comparison slide layout includes a title placeholder, two subtitle placeholders, and two content placeholders. If you want to include two tables that viewers can compare side by side, with a heading describing the contents of each, this is a useful layout to use.

The Table Tools Design tab is displayed.

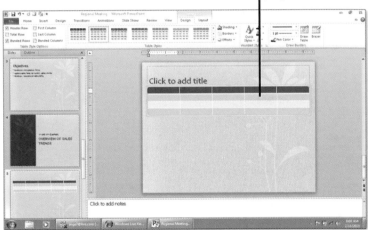

See Also

Although this section deals with the basics of inserting tables, please see "Editing Tables" on page 116 for more about formatting tables.

Insert Rows and Columns

① Click the table to select it.

② Click the Table Tools, Layout tab.

③ Place your mouse pointer above a column or to the left of a row until the pointer turns into an arrow, and then click to select the column or row.

④ Click the Insert Left or Insert Right button to insert a column to the left or right of the selected column.

⑤ Click the Insert Above or Insert Below button to insert a row above or below the selected row.

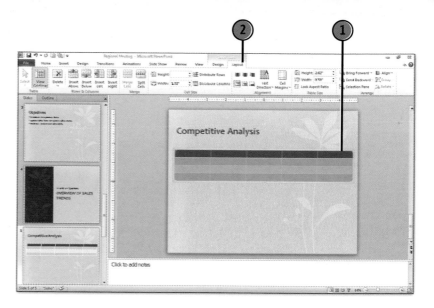

Tip

You can split the cells of a table column in two to include two sets of data without having to add a new column. Select the column as described in step 3 in the next task, and then click the Split Cells button on the Table Tools, Layout tab. In the Split Cells dialog box, click OK to accept the default number of columns. The column splits in two parts, and you can enter text in each.

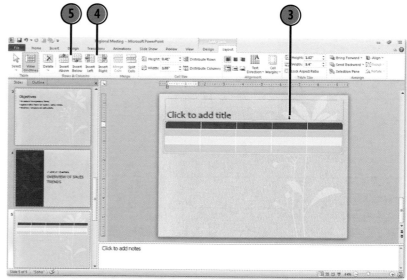

Editing Tables

There are several things you can do to help make your tables more easily readable, including adding borders to cells to keep the information separate and aligning text in cells both horizontally and vertically. You can also merge two or more cells. For example, you can merge cells so that the title of a table runs across all the columns in the table.

Modify Table Borders

1. Drag across a table to select all its cells.

2. Click the Table Tools, Design tab.

3. Click the arrow at the right side of the Borders tool.

4. Choose a border style such as All Borders to outline each and every cell in the table or Outside Borders to surround the outside of the table with a border.

Try This!

You can use the Draw Table tool to draw borders around cells one by one. Click the Draw Table tool on the Table Tools, Design tab. Then, using the pencil-shaped pointer, click any cell edge to draw a line. This method draws only one cell edge at a time. To get rid of a cell border, you can use the Erase tool on the same tab.

See Also

For information about formatting table styles and adding background colors, see "Formatting Objects" on page 149.

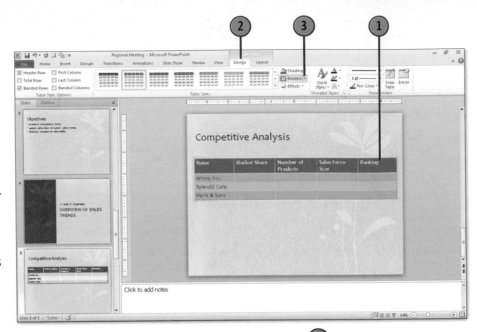

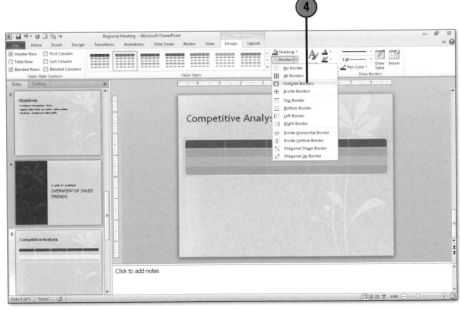

Align Text in Cells

① Drag across the cells to select the ones whose text you want to align.

② Click the Table Tools, Layout tab.

③ Click the Align Text Left, Center, or Align Text Right buttons to align the text from left to right in the cells.

④ Click the Align Top, Center Vertically, or Align Bottom buttons to align the text between the top and bottom of the cells.

Tip

You can also click the Arrange button on the Home tab, click Align, and then choose any of the alignment commands from the menu that appears.

Try This!

To align a table relative to the edges of your slides, click Arrange, Align, and choose Align To Slide.

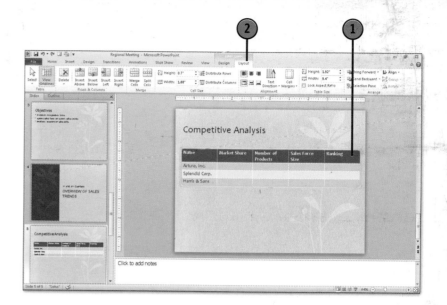

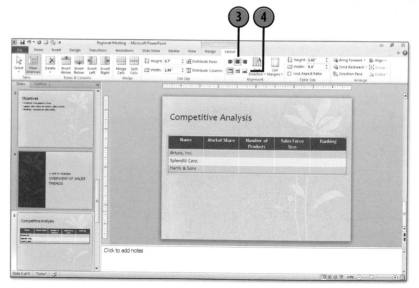

Merge Cells

1 Drag to select the cells you want to merge.

2 Click the Table Tools, Layout tab.

3 Click Merge Cells.

Try This!

To return the merged cells to individual cells again, drag to select the merged cell, and then click the Split Cells button on the Table Tools, Layout tab. In the dialog box that appears, enter the number of columns or rows you want to split the merged cell into, and click OK.

Tip

You can merge any number of cells, including cells in multiple rows and columns. This is often useful for tables you use to create forms that might have nonuniform cells for holding different types of information or pictures of various sizes.

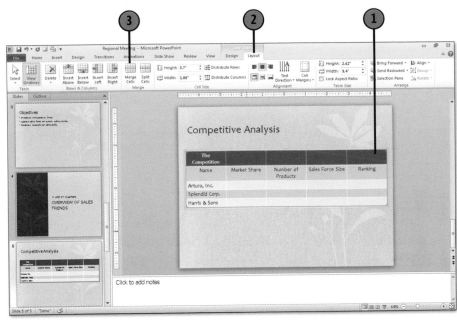

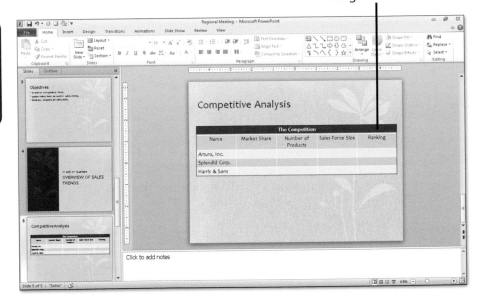

The selected cells are merged into one.

Creating and Modifying Charts

Charts in PowerPoint are based on Excel's charting feature. When you insert a chart, Excel opens so that you can enter the underlying data for the chart. When Excel opens, it displays some sample data, which should help you enter your specific data in the proper format to form the basis of a chart. Charts are wonderful tools for providing lots of information in a quickly understood, visual format. PowerPoint's chart feature offers dozens of styles of charts to choose from.

Insert a Chart

1. Click the Insert tab.
2. Click Chart.
3. Click a category of chart type on the left.
4. Click a chart style from the thumbnails displayed.
5. Click OK.

Try This!

You can also insert a chart by using the icons that appear in an empty content placeholder. Click the icon in the middle of the top row of icons to display the Create Chart dialog box, where you can specify the type and style of chart as outlined in the preceding steps.

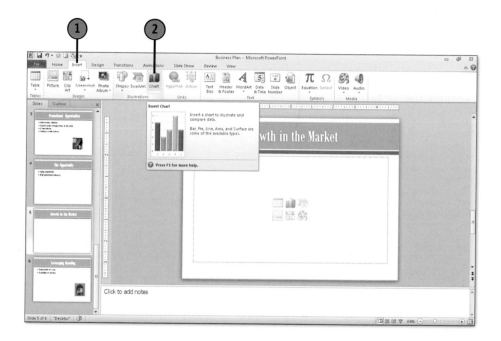

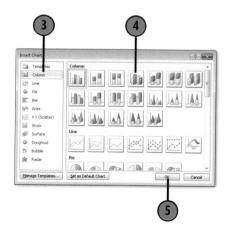

(6) Modify the sample data with your own source data for the chart.

(7) Click the Close button in the Excel window to return to PowerPoint and view the chart.

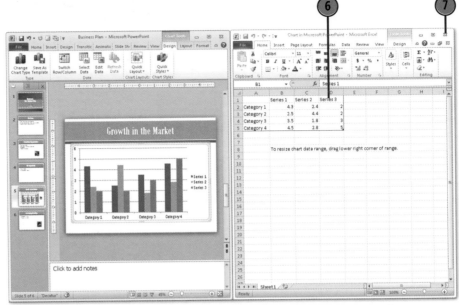

The chart appears on your PowerPoint slide.

Tip

You can change the chart type at any time by clicking Change Chart Type on the Chart Tools, Design tab. The Change Chart Type dialog box (which is identical to the Create Chart dialog box) appears for you to select another type of chart.

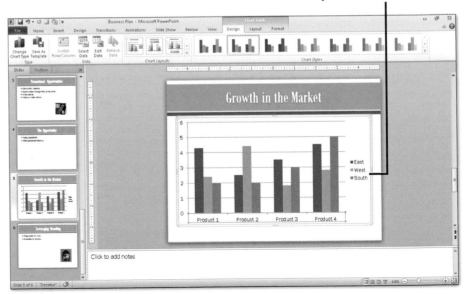

Change Chart Style and Layout

(1) Click a chart to select it.

(2) Click the Chart Tools, Design tab.

(3) Click the More button on the Chart Layouts gallery.

(4) Click a new layout to apply it.

(5) Click the More button on the Chart Styles gallery.

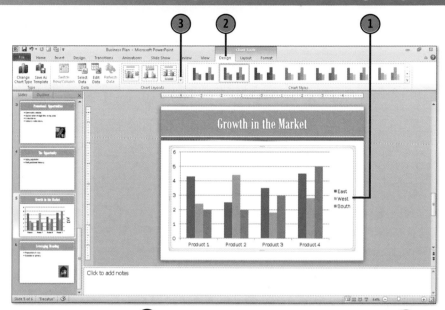

Tip

Chart types control the chart objects, such as whether your chart uses bars, lines, or pie wedges to represent data. Chart layouts control whether your chart includes a legend, the source data, and elements such as grid lines. The Chart Styles gallery offers sets of colors for chart elements and the chart background.

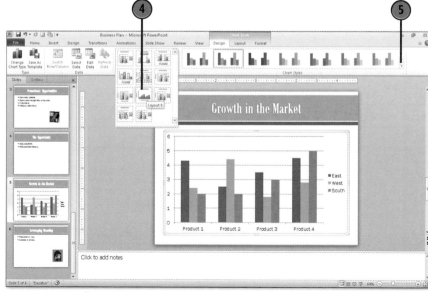

6 Click a new style to apply it.

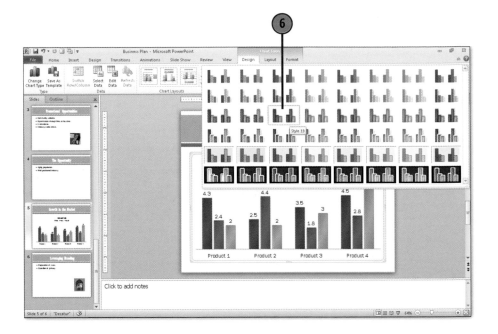

Tip

A layout applies formatting to your chart, but you can modify each aspect of the chart layout manually by using the tools on the Chart Tools, Layout tab. The next task explains how to modify the legend display, for example.

Display or Hide a Chart Legend

1 Click on a chart to select it.

2 Click the Chart Tools, Layout tab.

3 Click Legend.

Tip

Instead of choosing a placement for the legend by selecting a layout or by using the Legend button, you can move the legend to any position you want by dragging it within the chart box.

4 Click a layout position for the legend, or click None to turn the legend off.

Try This!

You can format a legend by right-clicking it in the chart and choosing Format Legend. In the Format Legend dialog box, you can modify the position of the legend and the line style surrounding it, add a fill color as a background for it, and so on.

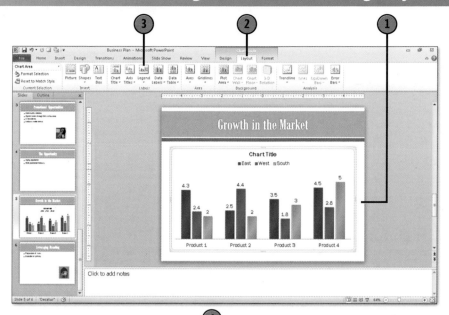

Inserting Clip Art

Clip art is a treasure trove of absolutely free art that you can use in your presentations to help get your message across or simply to add some visual excitement. Clip art includes photos, illustrations, movies, and sounds. PowerPoint comes with one collection of clip art, but you can also browse the Internet to access other collections. You can use the Clip Art task pane to search for and insert clip art.

Search for Clip Art

① With a slide layout containing a content placeholder displayed, click the Clip Art icon.

② Enter a search term in the Search For box to find related art.

③ Click the arrow on the Results Should Be list, and choose the format of media you want to search.

See Also

For information about rotating clip art objects, see "Rotating and Flipping Objects" on page 155.

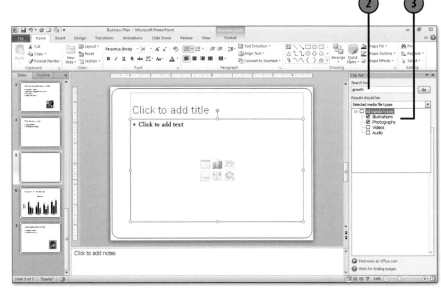

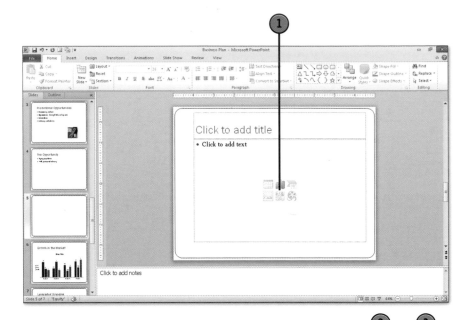

Caution

Although clip art is typically free, other art you find on the Internet is not. You must get permission to use any art or text you find online and sometimes must pay a fee. If you want additional free clip art, a safe bet is to go to Microsoft Office Online and browse for clip art collections.

(4) Click Go.

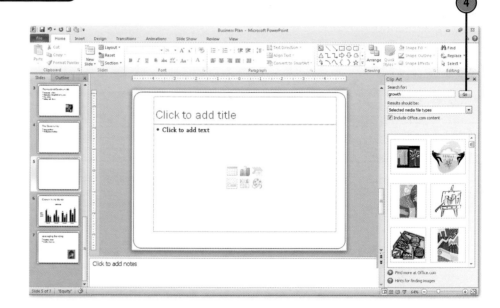

Tip

To view clip art collections available from the Microsoft Office Web site, you can select the Include Office.com Content check box under the Results Should Be list in the Clip Art task pane. You must be logged on to the Internet to view these collections.

Insert Clip Art

1 After performing a search for clip art, scroll through the results in the Clip Art task pane by using the scroll bar.

2 To insert a clip, click the thumbnail of the clip, or...

3 Click the arrow along the side of the clip and choose Insert.

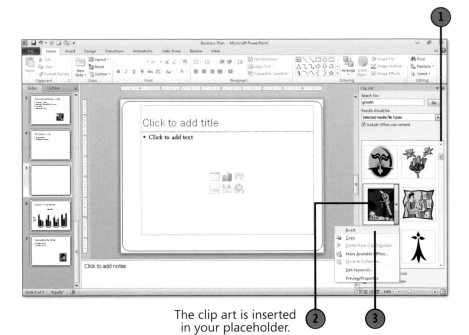

The clip art is inserted in your placeholder.

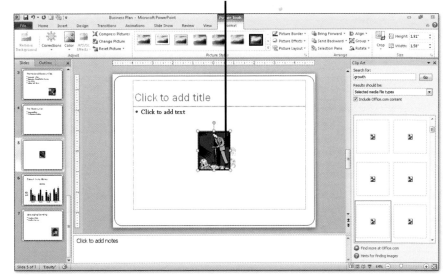

Creating WordArt

WordArt is a tool that allows you to apply interesting effects such as curves or 3-D views to any text. WordArt is best used to call attention to an important short phrase, such as "Free!" or "All New." The distortions of WordArt designs can make longer phrases hard to read. You first insert a WordArt placeholder, then enter text into it, and then apply various effects.

Insert WordArt

① Click the Insert tab.

② Click WordArt.

③ Click a WordArt style.

④ Type your text in the placeholder.

Try This!

You can also select text in your presentation and then follow the steps to insert WordArt. In this case, the WordArt placeholder appears with the selected text already displayed in it.

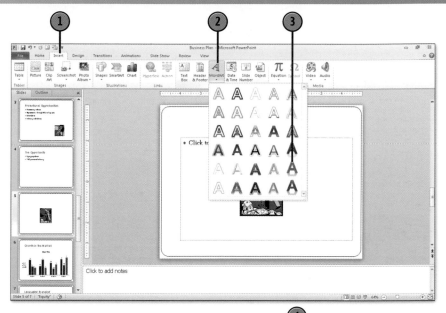

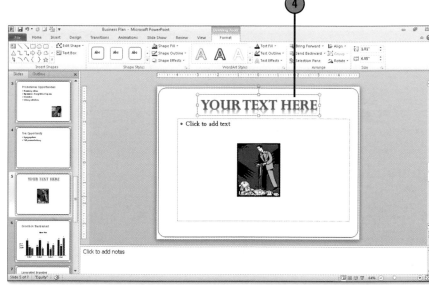

5 Click outside the placeholder to view the WordArt.

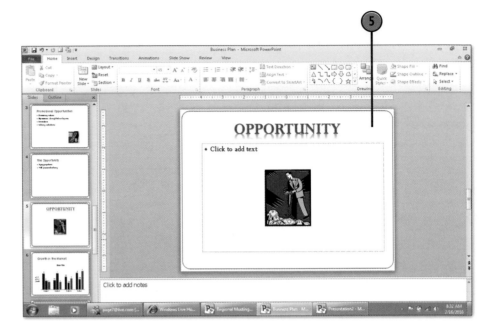

Tip

You can resize WordArt easily by clicking a handle around the edges and dragging out or in. To keep the object's original proportions, be sure to drag only a corner handle.

Apply Effects to WordArt

1. Click the WordArt object to select it.

2. Click the Drawing Tools, Format tab.

3. Click Shape Effects.

Tip

In versions of PowerPoint prior to Microsoft Office 2007, you chose one set of effects, such as shape, 3-D perspective, and colors, to apply to your WordArt. In PowerPoint 2010 and 2007, WordArt offers more powerful design tools, although you have to apply various effects individually. You can use the Shape Effects, Shape Outline, and Shape Fill tools on the Drawing Tools, Format tab to individually apply these effects. You can also use the QuickStyles gallery to choose preset combinations of effects.

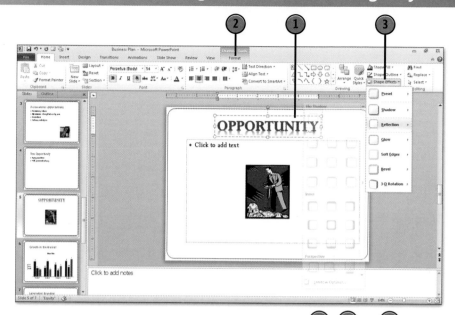

4. Move your mouse pointer over a category, and another gallery appears.

5. Move your pointer over various effects to preview them on your WordArt object.

6. Click an effect, and it's applied to the WordArt. You can apply multiple categories of effects.

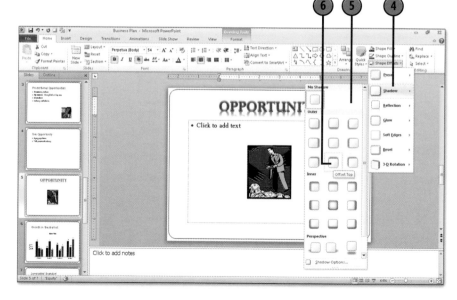

Working with SmartArt

A feature that was new in PowerPoint 2007 and is also in PowerPoint 2010 is SmartArt, a souped-up diagramming tool that allows you to quickly create all kinds of diagrams and workflow charts. After you select and insert a SmartArt diagram, you can use a simple outline pane to enter the text that populates the various boxes and shapes in the diagram. You can insert or delete elements easily. SmartArt also works like the shapes built into PowerPoint, so after you insert a diagram, you can change various elements of it by altering its shapes, adding shapes, modifying their colors, and more.

Insert SmartArt

1. Display a slide with a layout containing a content placeholder.

2. Click the SmartArt icon in the placeholder (in the top-right corner).

3. In the Choose A SmartArt Graphic dialog box, click a category on the left.

4. Click a style in the center.

5. Click OK to insert the SmartArt object.

Tip

You can close the text entry box to the left of a SmartArt object by clicking the Close button in the top-right corner. To redisplay it, click the left-facing arrow along the left side of the SmartArt object.

Tip

Some SmartArt styles include picture icons. Click these to display the Insert Picture dialog box. Locate a picture file you want to use, and click Insert. This feature is useful for diagrams such as organizational charts in which you want to insert photos of individuals in the organization.

See Also

For more information about working with objects on your slides, see "Formatting Objects" on page 149.

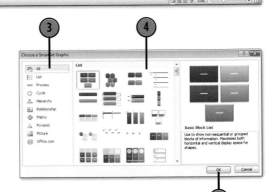

Add Text to SmartArt

1 Click the SmartArt placeholder to open it for editing.

2 Type the text for the first heading

3 Click in the next text box, and type the next heading.

4 Headings appear in the SmartArt graphic. Press the Up or Down arrow key to move between headings, and then continue to fill in the headings. If you want to add an additional heading, press Enter after typing a heading.

Tip

To insert SmartArt in a placeholder that doesn't contain content icons, just click the Insert tab and then click the SmartArt button to insert SmartArt anywhere on the slide.

Tip

The Tab key works a little differently in SmartArt. If you press Tab after clicking a heading placeholder, the cursor does not move to the next heading as it does in some forms and programs. Instead, if you click a heading placeholder and press Tab, the heading is indented one level. If you click a heading and press Shift+Tab, the heading moves up one level in the outline.

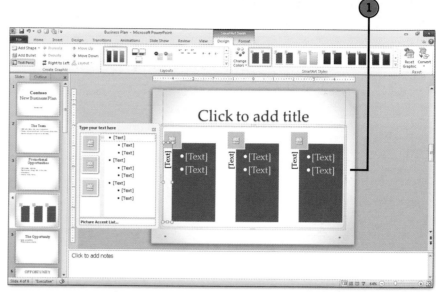

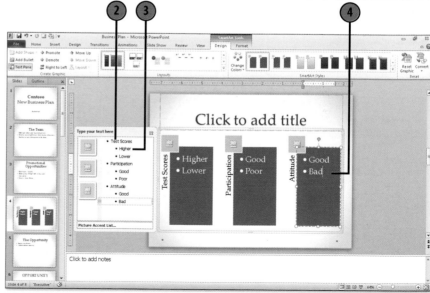

Working with Pictures

If you have taken photos yourself or somebody has provided photos, using them in PowerPoint can add to your presentation's impact. Perhaps you have a photo of your newest product for a sales presentation, or a photo of your soccer team in action for a school sports presentation. Inserting a photo onto a slide is easy to do. Once a picture is inserted, you can trim away unwanted portions by using the Crop tool.

Insert a Picture

① Display a slide with a layout that contains a content placeholder.

② Click the Insert Picture From File icon.

See Also

The Photo Album feature allows you to create groups of photos to help you organize your images. For more about this feature, see "Creating a Photo Album" on page 137.

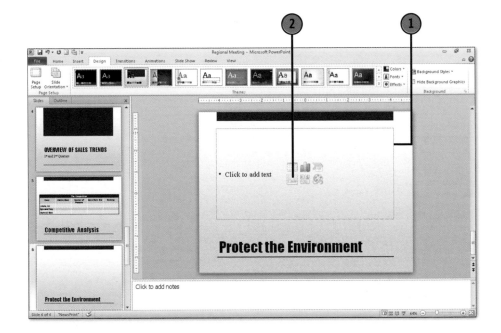

(3) Locate the picture file you want to insert, and click it to select it.

(4) Click Insert.

Tip

Insert a picture anywhere on a slide by clicking the Picture button on the Insert tab.

See Also

For more information about formatting pictures by using the Picture Tools, Format tab on the ribbon, see "Working with Picture Tools" on page 160.

The picture appears on the slide.

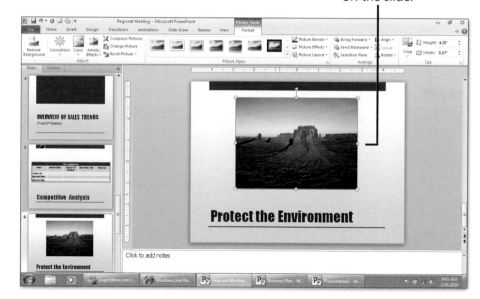

Crop a Picture

1. Click a picture to select it.
2. Click the Picture Tools, Format tab.
3. Click Crop.

Tip

If you just want a smaller picture, you can resize it rather than remove some of the picture by cropping. To resize a picture, select it, click any of the handles that appear, and then drag in or out.

4. Click any of the lines that appear around the edge of the picture, and then drag inward to crop the picture. Continue cropping from various sides until the picture appears as you want it to.

5. Press the Esc key, or click anywhere outside the picture to turn off the Crop tool.

Tip

If you crop too much from your picture, you can use the Crop tool to drag outward again and restore the portion you cropped. You can do this even after deactivating the cropping session in which you first trimmed the picture.

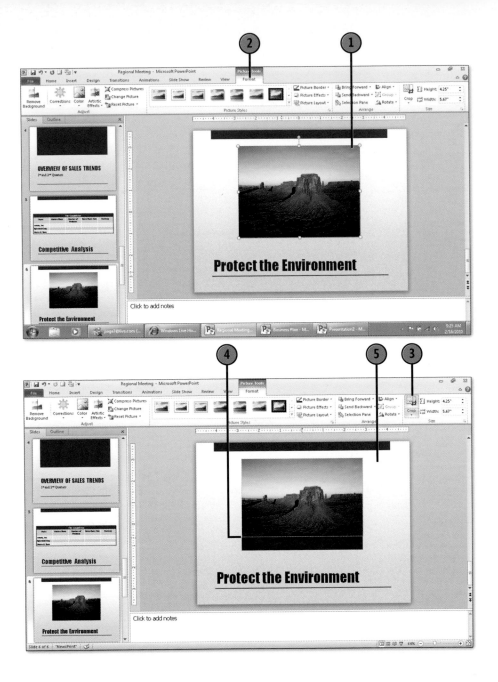

Inserting Media Objects

Sprinkling sounds and video into your presentations can add some sparkle or even help you bring a point home with flair. When you insert multimedia objects onto slides, a video object is indicated by an illustration icon, and an audio object is indi- cated by a small speaker icon. You can choose to play the video or sound object as soon as the slide it's placed on appears or when you click the object while running in Slide Show view.

Insert Video or Audio

① Click the Insert tab.

② Click the Video or Audio button.

Tip

You can also insert a media clip from the Clip Art task pane. When searching for clip art, just select Videos or Audio in the Results Should Be list. By inserting a media clip in this way, you can use a preview feature to see or hear it before inserting the object. See "Inserting Clip Art" on page 124 for more about how to do this.

③ Locate the file you want to insert, and click Insert.

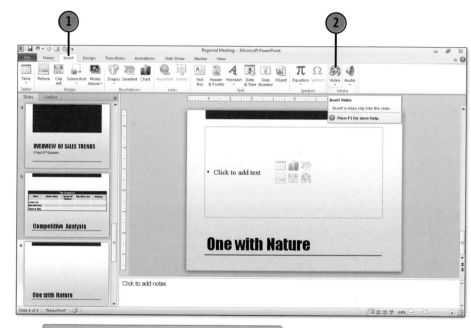

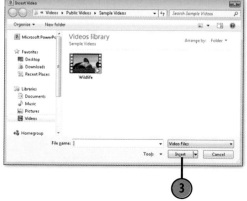

4 Click the Play/Pause button in the toolbar beneath the media icon to preview the file.

5 Click the Video/Audio Tools, Playback tab, and then click Automatically or On Click to select how you want the object to run.

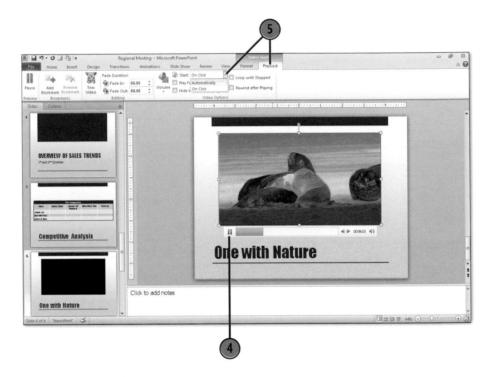

Tip

If you set up a media clip to play automatically when a slide appears during a slide show, it plays once. If you want to play it again, you can click the object to start it over.

Creating a Photo Album

If you want to create a slide show or a portion of a show that consists of a series of photos, you can use a feature called Photo Album. A photo album is a tool you use to set up a series of photos and text boxes, one each per slide in sequence. You can include captions for the photos, and you can also make use of photo editing tools included in the Photo Album feature. These tools allow you to rotate photos or change their brightness or contrast.

Insert a New Photo Album

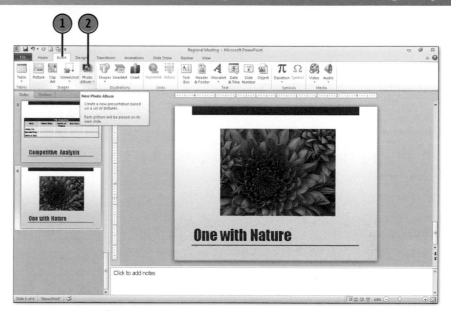

1. Click the Insert tab.

2. Click Photo Album.

3. Click the File/Disk button in the Photo Album dialog box.

4. Locate a picture to insert, and then click the Insert button. Repeat this for as many photos as you want to include in the album.

Try This!

You can edit a photo album once you've created it. Click the arrow on the Photo Album button, and then choose Edit Photo Album. In the Edit Photo Album dialog box, use the tools to remove photos, add photos, rearrange photos, or change any of the picture or layout options.

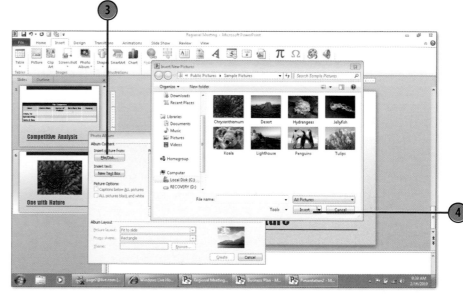

⑤ If you want to include a text slide, click the New Text Box button.

⑥ Use any of the tools to modify your photo album.

⑦ Click Create to save the album. The new presentation is created. Save it as a stand-alone presentation or insert it into a larger presentation.

See Also

After you create a photo album, you can modify the individual pictures by resizing, rotating, or moving them on the slides. For more information about working with objects, see "Rotating and Flipping Objects" on page 155.

Click to select picture options such as using captions or showing all photos in black and white.

Click the Up and Down arrow buttons to change the sequence of photos.

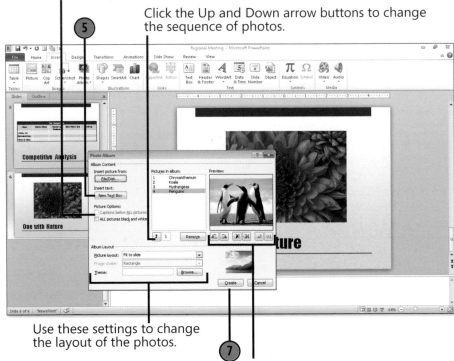

Use these settings to change the layout of the photos.

Use these tools to rotate the image or adjust the brightness or contrast.

Drawing Shapes and Text Boxes

You can use the Shapes feature in PowerPoint to draw a variety of objects—from lines, arrows, and boxes to scrolls, callouts, and action buttons. When you draw a shape, you can enter text in it; however, that text does not appear in your presentation outline. If you draw an action button, you can then associate an action with that button, such as running another program or playing a sound when you click the button during a slide show. In addition to various shapes, you can draw a text box, which is simply a placeholder where you can enter text. By default, a text box has no border, so the text appears to float on your page. Text in text boxes is not reflected in the presentation outline.

Draw a Shape

① Click the Insert tab.

② Click Shapes.

③ Click a shape. Your mouse pointer turns into a plus sign.

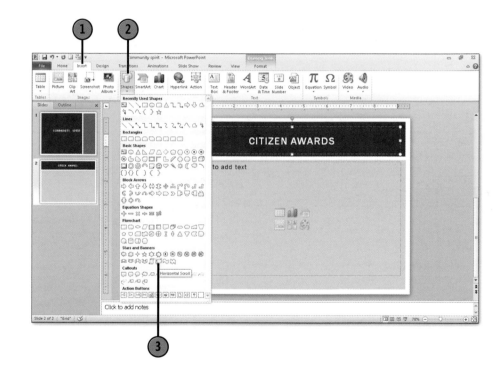

④ Click anywhere on your slide, and then drag to draw an object of whatever size you need.

⑤ If you draw an action button, a dialog box appears in which you can choose to jump to another slide or presentation, run a program, run a macro, initiate an action, or play a sound. Make the settings you need.

⑥ Click OK to save the settings.

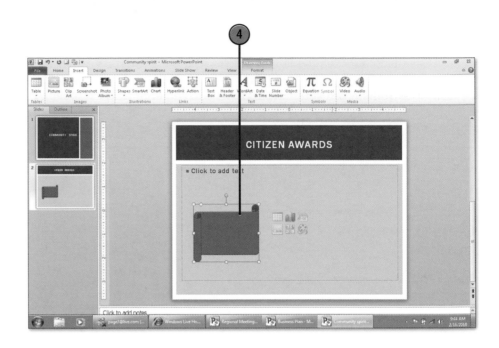

Try This!

You can use an action button setting to link to a URL. With your computer connected to the Internet, this allows you to display a Web site during your presentation. Use this feature to show your company's Web site or to bring up an image or data on another site to help support your presentation's point.

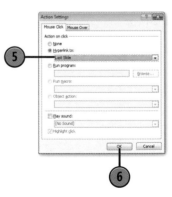

Tip

There are two tabs in the Action Settings dialog box, Mouse Click and Mouse Over. Depending on which tab you use to make settings, the action is initiated when you click the object or when you pass your mouse over the object during the presentation.

Tip

After you draw a shape on your slide, you can just click it and begin typing to add text.

Add a Text Box

1 Click the Insert tab.

2 Click Text Box. Your pointer turns into a plus sign.

3 Drag on the slide to draw the text box, which remains open for editing.

4 Type text, and then click outside the box.

Tip

You can format a text box. Right-click the text, and choose Format Shape. In the Format Shape dialog box, use the various categories of settings to add fill color, an outside border, 3-D and rotation effects, and more. When you select a shape you've drawn, the Drawing Tools, Format tab becomes available, which you can also use to make formatting changes.

See Also

In addition to adding action buttons to your slides, you can use effects such as animations and transitions to make your presentation more dynamic. See Section 12, "Adding Transitions and Animations," starting on page 167, for more about working with animations and transitions on slides.

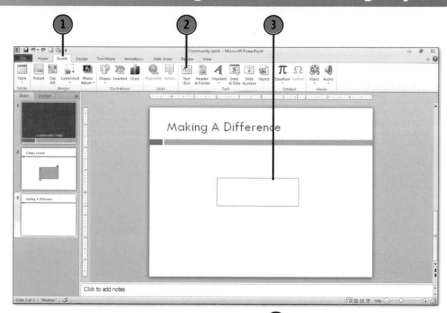

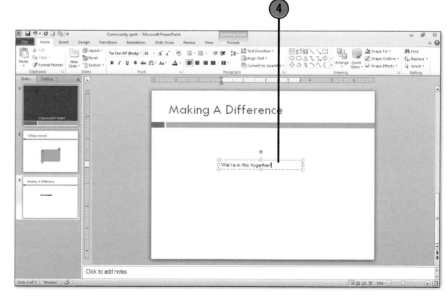

Formatting Text, Objects, and Slides

If you select a theme for your slides, a set of font styles and colors are applied, but sometimes you might want to modify those styles or format a portion of the text for emphasis.

In addition to formatting text, placing a picture, a piece of line art, or a drawing on a slide helps you add some interest to your presentation, but it's important that you make the object fit your overall design. That might mean resizing or rotating the object to align it better with other elements on the slide, or you might need to modify the color or brightness of an image to match your slide color scheme.

It may be useful to group objects that you insert on your slide so that you can move or modify them as one object, or to set an order for objects so that one appears on top of another if they overlap.

Finally, Microsoft PowerPoint 2010 provides tools you can use to customize pictures and videos that you place in your presentation and slide backgrounds that you choose for one or more of your slides.

In this section, you explore the many ways you can format text and objects in PowerPoint and learn how to resize, rotate, group, and order those objects.

Applying Fonts

Fonts are sets of design styles for text, and they add a distinct personality to your slide contents. Some fonts are playful, others are traditional, and still others are great for adding emphasis. The trick to choosing the right font for a presentation is to be sure that it fits the design mood of your slides.

You should also be sure that it is readable by your audience in whatever setting you show your presentation.

Select a Font

1. Click the Home tab.

2. Select the text you want to format.

3. Click the arrow on the Font list.

4. Move your mouse pointer down the list of fonts. Each font is previewed on the selected text in turn as you move the pointer through the list.

5. Click the font you want to apply to the selected text.

Tip ✓

The fonts you see on the Font list are those that are installed with Windows. You can find additional font sets online, some free and some that you have to pay for. Visit the Microsoft Typography Web site at *www.microsoft.com/ typography/default.mspx* to learn more about fonts and to find additional font sets.

Try This!

You can also use the Font dialog box to change the font; however, there is no preview of the font's appearance using this method. Click the dialog box launcher in the Font group on the Home tab to open the dialog box, and then click the arrow in the Latin Text Font list to display the Font list. Choose the font you want, and then click OK to apply it to selected text. The main benefit of using the Font dialog box is that you can apply several formatting settings, such as size, font, and a bold effect, from one location.

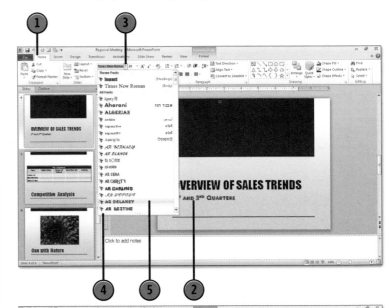

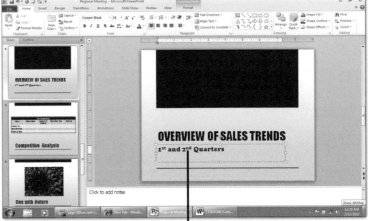

The font is applied to your selection.

Formatting Text

There are several things you can do to help make your text more interesting or more easily readable, including resizing it, changing its color, or applying effects such as bold, italic, or underline. Design themes apply preset font size and color, but when you want to fit more text on a page or emphasize some text, resizing is handy. When you want to call attention to certain text, changing its color or making it bold, for example, can make it stand out.

Change Text Color

1 Click the Home tab.

2 Select the text you want to format.

3 Click the Font Color tool.

4 Move your mouse pointer over the colors in the palette to preview them in the selected text.

Tip

Be careful about choosing lighter colors that are hard to read unless your slides have a dark background against which a light color can stand out. Likewise, don't choose dark font colors to use against a dark background. Remember, the whole point of your presentation is that viewers should be able to read it!

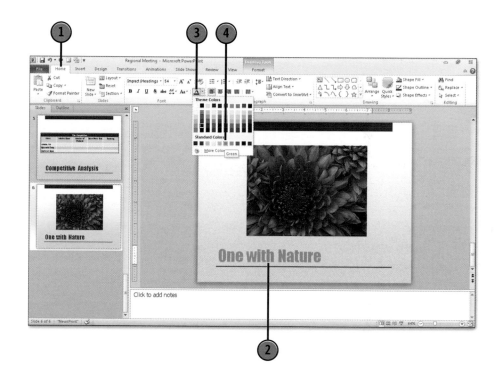

5 Click the More Colors option to view additional color choices.

6 Click either the Standard or Custom tab.

7 Click a color choice. The Custom tab offers a red-green-blue (RGB) color system that provides many more color choices and lets you make specific RGB settings.

8 Click OK to close the Color dialog box, and apply the new color.

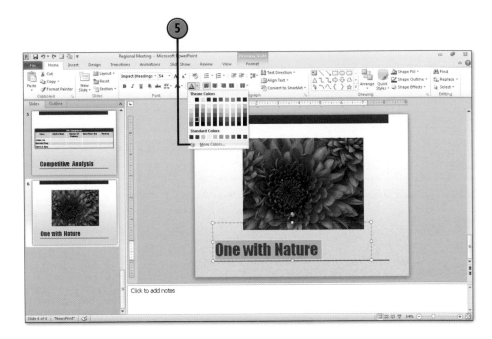

Tip

You can use the contextual toolbar that appears when you select text to change the font size and color or apply effects.

See Also

To change the background color of your slides so that it works with your font color choices, see "Changing the Slide Background" on page 165.

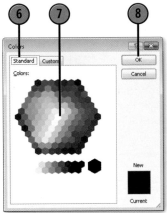

Change Text Size

(1) Click the Home tab.

(2) Select the text you want to resize.

(3) Click the arrow on the Font Size tool.

(4) Move your pointer over the sizes, and they are previewed on the selected text.

(5) Click a size to apply it.

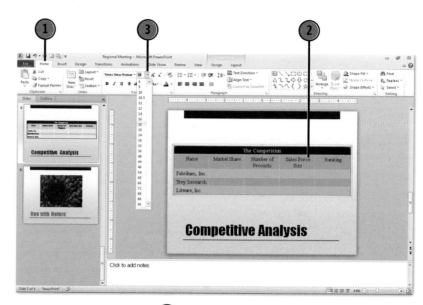

Try This!

Not every single font size is available on the Font Size list. Only very commonly used sizes are included. If you find you need a size in between the preset ones, you can also type a size, such as 100, 13, or 30, in the Font Size box to apply it.

Tip

Don't make fonts so small that they are difficult to read. Also, notice that as you add text to a placeholder, font sizes might shrink to fit in all the text. By keeping font sizes large enough to read and your placeholder text to no more than six or so short bullet points, you ensure that your viewers can see your presentation contents clearly.

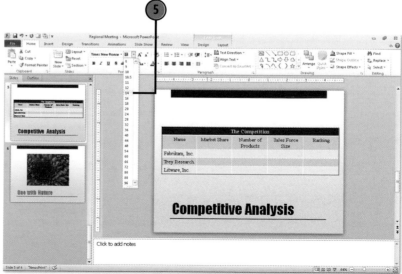

Apply Effects to Text

① Click the Home tab.

② Select the text you want to format.

③ Click any of the following buttons to apply that format to the selected text:

- Bold
- Underline
- Shadow
- Italic
- Strikethrough

④ Click the arrow on the Character Spacing button.

⑤ Click the spacing you prefer, from Very Tight to Very Loose. Very tight spacing pushes letters close together; very loose spacing places them farther apart.

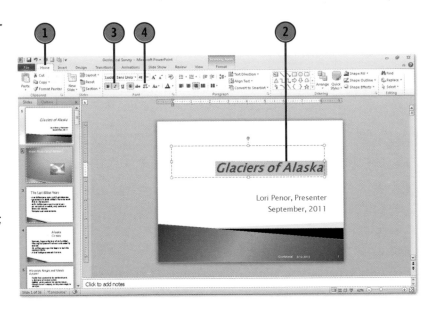

Try This!

To create custom character spacing, click the More Spacing option on the Character Spacing list. In the Font dialog box that appears, on the Character Spacing tab choose Expanded or Condensed from the Spacing list, and then specify by how many points this effect should be applied. Click OK to save the new setting.

Tip

Character spacing is also known as kerning. On the Character Spacing tab in the Font dialog box, you can specify that the kerning you apply be used only for fonts of a certain size or larger by selecting the Kerning For Fonts check box and selecting a font size.

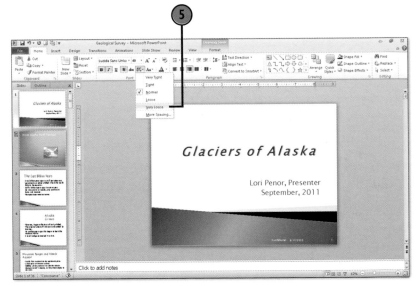

Tip

You can apply multiple effects to text, such as bold plus italic plus shadow, but don't go overboard, or you'll make the text too busy to read!

Formatting Objects

Objects, including clip art, WordArt, pictures, and shapes that you draw on your slides, can all be formatted in several ways. You can fill an object with color or a pattern, change the outline of the shape by modifying the line style and thickness, and apply a wide variety of effects, such as softening the edges or applying a three-dimensional (3-D) or rotation effect. Together, these formatting options let you customize an object to make it appear just the way you want it to.

Apply a Fill Color or Effect

1 Select a shape, text box, or WordArt object. (You can also perform these steps with SmartArt objects, but the Format tab in the next step is then named SmartArt Tools.)

2 Click the Drawing Tools, Format tab.

3 Click the Shape Fill button.

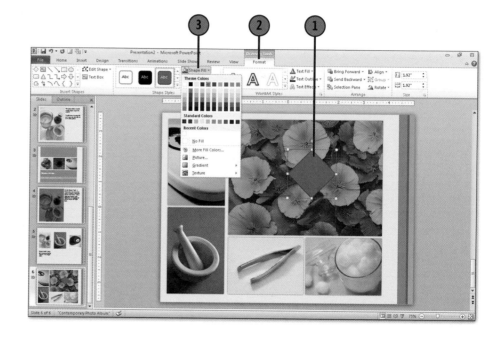

4 Use the Shape Fill gallery to make the changes you want to the selected object.

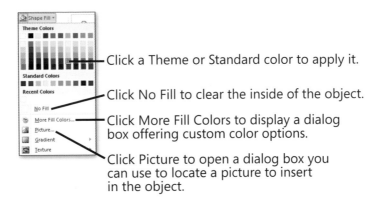

Click a Theme or Standard color to apply it.

Click No Fill to clear the inside of the object.

Click More Fill Colors to display a dialog box offering custom color options.

Click Picture to open a dialog box you can use to locate a picture to insert in the object.

Click Gradient or Texture to display a submenu of choices.

Try This!

The Fill gallery uses the Live Preview feature. When you pass your mouse pointer over a Theme or Standard color or over a Gradient or Texture option, it is previewed on the object on your slide.

Tip

You cannot add a fill to clip art or a picture object because their "fill" is the image they contain. However, you can change their shape or border or add effects such as 3-D. See tasks elsewhere in this section to learn how to do this.

Change the Shape Outline

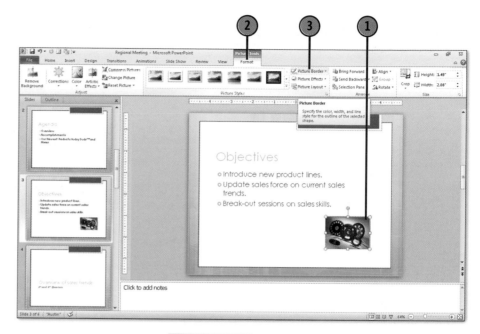

(1) Click an object to select it.

(2) Click the Drawing/Picture Tools, Format tab (depending on whether you've selected a picture or other type of object).

(3) Click the Picture Border or Shape Outline button.

(4) Use the gallery to make the changes you want to the selected object.

- Click More Outline Colors to display a dialog box offering custom color options.

- Click Weight, Dashes, or Arrows (drawing objects only) to display a submenu of formatting choices for the picture border or shape outline.

- Click No Outline to clear any outline or border.

- Click a Theme or Standard color to apply it as the outline or border.

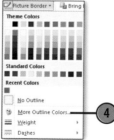

Tip

The Arrow option on the Shape Outline or Picture Border palette is available only if you are working with a line object.

See Also

If you want to format a placeholder rather than an object, see "Formatting Placeholders" on page 80.

Apply a Shape Effect

1. Click an object to select it.

2. Click the Drawing Tools/Picture Tools, Format tab (depending on the type of object you selected).

3. Click the Shape Effects or Picture Effects button.

4. Move your mouse pointer over a category of effects, and then click on an effect in the gallery that appears.

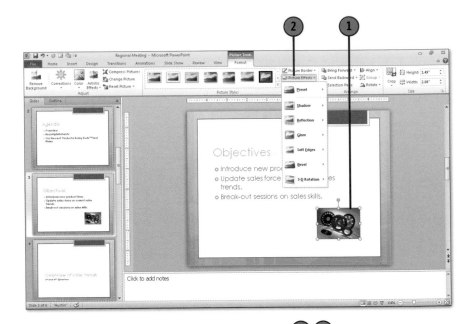

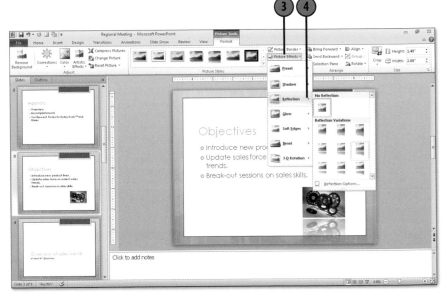

Repeat steps 3 and 4 to apply additional effects to the object.

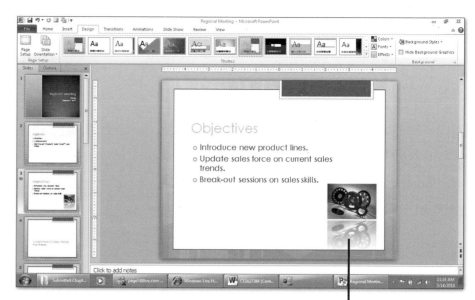

The effect is applied.

Tip

You can apply more than one effect to an object. For example, you might choose to add a shadow, a reflection, and a 3-D effect to one image. Just remember that you have to apply these effects one by one, using the steps outlined here.

Try This!

You can click the Format Shape dialog box launcher in the Shape Styles group to open the Format Shape dialog box. From there you can apply all kinds of effects to the selected object from one place. When you are done applying effects, click Close, and they are all applied.

Resizing Objects

When you insert an object, it may not fit exactly as you'd like alongside other objects or placeholders on your slide. In that case, you can resize the object easily by using resizing handles that appear when you click the object. Dragging corner handles resizes the object while maintaining its original proportions. Dragging handles on the sides of the object resizes it but does not maintain the original proportions. This can cause it to appear distorted, like an image in a funhouse mirror.

Resize Objects

1. Click the object you want to resize.

2. Click a handle, and then drag inward to shrink the object or drag outward to enlarge it.

3. To resize the object to a specific measurement, click the Format tab.

4. In the Size group, use the arrows for the Shape Height and Shape Width settings to specify a measurement.

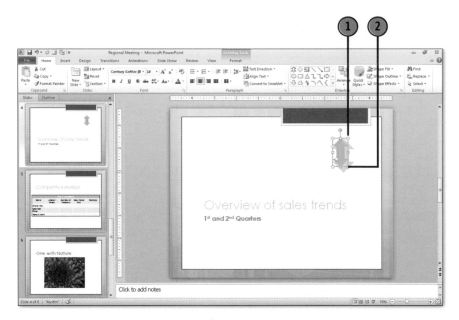

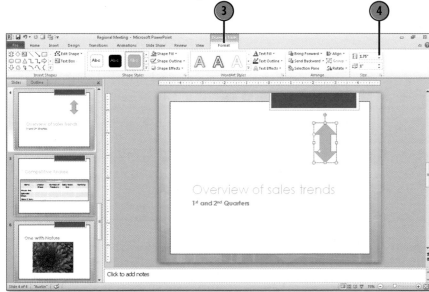

See Also

Sometimes rotating an object helps you fit it on a slide among other objects. See the next task, "Rotating and Flipping Objects," to learn how to rotate an object.

Tip

If a picture is too large for your slide, consider cropping it by using the Crop tool on the Format tab. This allows you to trim out unneeded portions of the picture, thereby saving space, without reducing the picture size, which might make it hard to see. For more about working with pictures, see Section 10, "Inserting Media and Drawing Objects," starting on page 113.

Rotating and Flipping Objects

Being able to rotate objects can help you make interesting design arrangements on your slides or help organize objects so that they fit together. Rotating is easy to do using a rotation handle that appears whenever you click an object. By dragging the handle, you can rotate the object anywhere along a 360-degree axis.

Rotate an Object

1. Click the object to select it. Notice the green rotation handle that appears above it.

2. Drag the rotation handle to spin the object. When the object appears at the angle you want, release the mouse button.

3. To rotate the selected object precisely 90 degrees, click the Home tab.

4. Click the arrow on the Arrange button.

5. Click Rotate, and choose Rotate Right 90° or Rotate Left 90° from the submenu.

See Also

You can apply 3-D rotation effects to give objects perspective—as if they were rotated to place one edge farther in space from you than the other. See the task "Apply a Shape Effect" on page 152 to learn how to apply 3-D effects.

Tip

For more rotation options, click More Rotation Options on the Rotate menu. On the Size page in the Format Picture dialog box that appears, you can enter specific measurements for height and width as well as for setting the distance of the object from the edges of the slide.

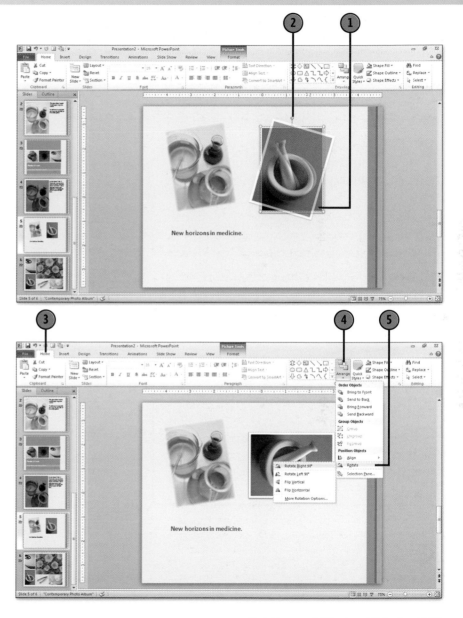

Flip an Object

(1) Select the object, and click the Home tab.

(2) Click the Arrange button.

(3) Click Rotate, and choose Flip Vertical or Flip Horizontal from the submenu. The action is previewed on the slide.

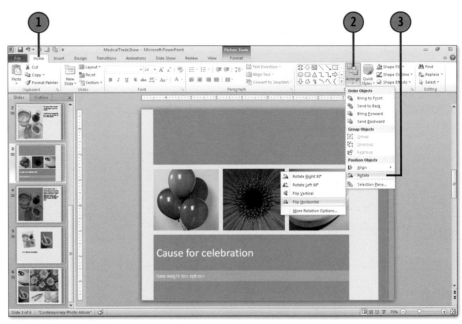

Tip

Flipping shifts the object precisely 180 degrees. Another way to precisely place an object on your slide is to use the rotation handle to freely rotate it, but to display the gridlines so that you end up with the object aligned precisely to the edge of the slide and not at an angle. To display gridlines, click the View tab, and select the Gridlines check box.

The object is flipped 180 degrees.

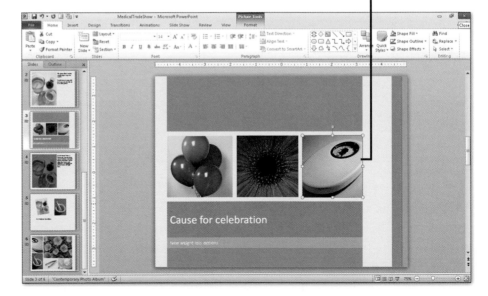

Grouping and Changing the Order of Objects

Two handy functions help you work with objects on your slide. Grouping allows you to group several objects, such as the different objects that form a drawing or logo, into a single object. You can then work with that single object to format, move, or resize it. Also, you might decide to have several objects on a slide overlap each other, either to save space or to create a design effect. In that case you should know how to control the order of objects on a page—that is, which object appears on top and which appears to be positioned underneath another.

Group and Ungroup Objects

1. Click an object to select it.

2. Press Ctrl, and then click on one or more other objects you want to group together.

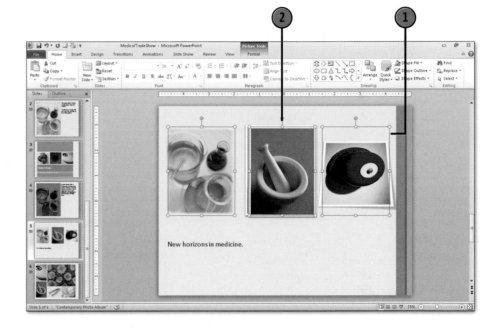

(3) Click the Drawing Tools, Format tab or Picture Tools, Format tab, depending on the type of object.

(4) Click the Group button, and choose Group.

(5) To ungroup the objects, select the grouped object, click the Group button, and then click Ungroup.

Tip

A grouped object has one outline surrounding all the objects and a single rotation handle. After objects are grouped, you can resize, move, rotate, and change the fill color of all objects at once.

Tip

To quickly select multiple objects on a slide, drag across them; a highlighted box surrounds the objects. Release your mouse, and all objects within the area you highlighted are selected (not including placeholders).

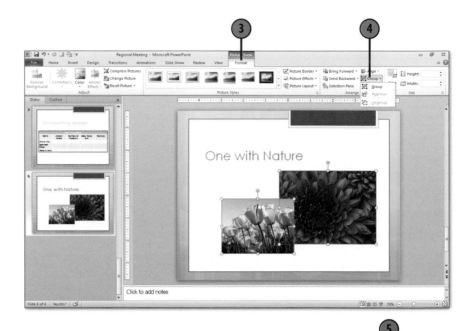

Change Object Order

(1) Click an object to select it.

(2) Click the Drawing Tools, Format tab or Picture Tools, Format tab, depending on the type of object you're working with.

(3) Click the Bring Forward or Send Backward button to move the object one place forward or back in any series of objects it overlaps.

See Also

For more information about inserting objects on your slides, see Section 10.

Tip

You can click the arrow on either the Bring Forward or Send Backward button and choose Bring to Front or Send to Back if you want to move an object all the way forward or backward in a stack of objects, rather than moving it one position at a time in the stack.

Working with Picture Tools

Because pictures have attributes such as brightness and contrast, they have their own special set of tools you can use to make adjustments to the images. By using these tools, you can make pictures that are too dark appear brighter and pictures that are hard to see crisper by adjusting the contrast between darks and lights. You can also recolor pictures to apply a wash of light or dark color to them.

Adjust Brightness or Contrast

1. Click a picture to select it.

2. Click the Picture Tools, Format tab.

3. Click Corrections.

4. Choose an option in the Brightness and Contrast section of the drop-down gallery or in the Sharpen and Soften section. The effects are previewed on the picture as you move your pointer over the options.

If you want to explore some interesting effects for your picture, such as adding granularity to the photo or washing away details to make it appear more like a drawing, click the Artistic Effects button, and move your mouse pointer over the effects displayed to preview them.

The Photo Album feature was introduced in PowerPoint 2007. It allows you to create groups of photos to help you organize your images. See "Creating a Photo Album" on page 137 for more about Photo Album.

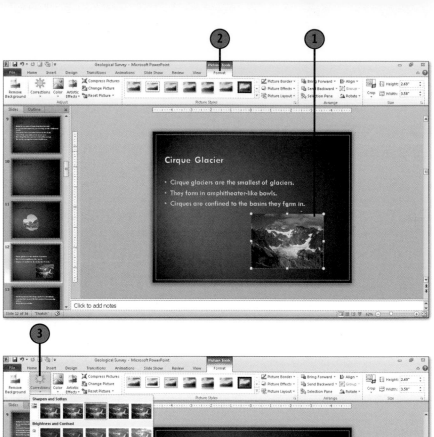

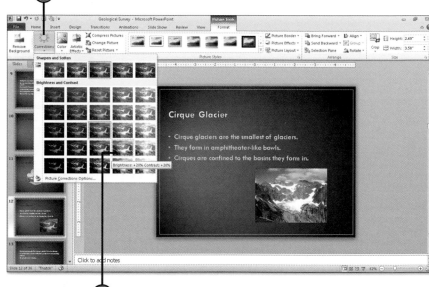

Recolor a Picture

1. Click a picture to select it.

2. Click the Picture Tools, Format tab.

3. Click Color.

4. Move your pointer to any Color Saturation, Color Tone, or Recolor option to preview it.

5. Click an option to apply it.

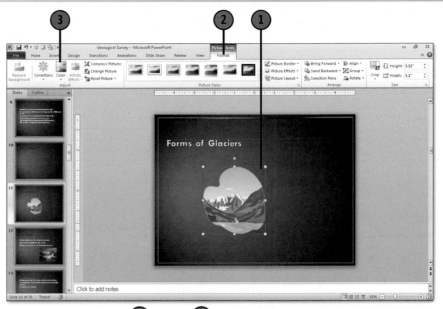

Tip

When you click Set Transparent Color on the Color menu, the portion of the image that you drag over with your mouse appears to disappear, revealing any objects underneath.

Caution

Be careful how you recolor pictures. Although coloring a picture can add some interest, it can also make the picture difficult to see in certain settings. Consider instead applying a colored border or slide background to add visual interest to a picture.

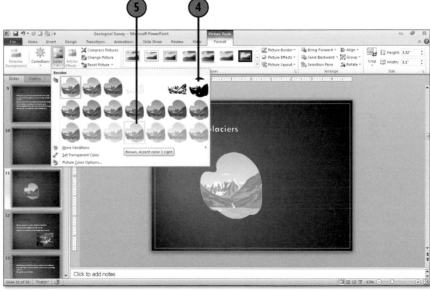

Using Video Tools

Not to be left behind in the age of video sharing sites such as YouTube, PowerPoint 2010 now offers enhanced video formatting tools. Video is a great way to add some multimedia punch to a presentation. Once you insert a video into a presentation, you can use these tools to format the shape and border of your video, modify playback options such as how playback is initiated, or even trim the video to get rid of unwanted footage. (See Section 10 for more about inserting video clips.)

Apply Video Formats

1. Click a video object to select it.

2. Click the Video Tools, Format tab.

3. Click the More arrow at the right of the Video Styles gallery.

4. Move your mouse pointer over the styles to preview them on your video clip. When you find one you like, click it.

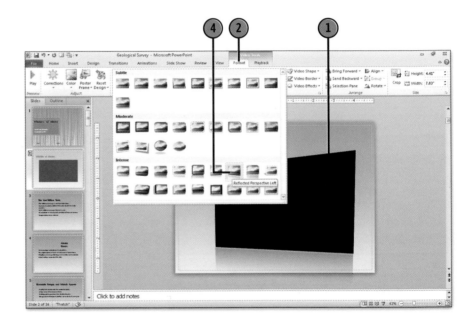

⑤ Click the Video Border tool, and select a color from the list to change the color of the border.

⑥ Click the Video Effects button, and choose from the variety of effects offered there.

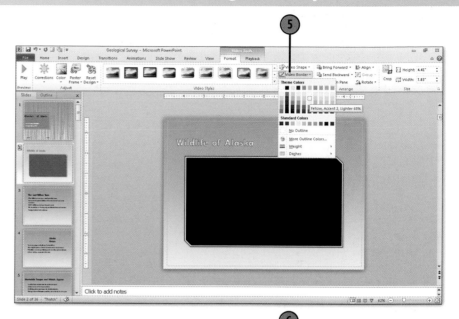

Tip

You can use the Corrections and Color buttons on the Format tab to modify the appearance of your video. These work similarly to the same tools covered under the previous task, "Working with Picture Tools."

Setting up Video Playback

1. Click a video object to select it.

2. Click the Video Tools, Playback tab.

3. In the Video Options group, click the arrow on the Start field, and choose whether the video should play automatically when you display the slide or manually when you click the video object.

4. Select various check boxes to set whether to play the video in full-screen mode, loop the video to play continuously, or rewind the video after it finishes playing.

5. Click Volume, and choose the volume for the video sound.

Tip ✓

If you want to trim the video to cut some of the footage from it, click the Trim Video button, and drag the left or right side of the bar at the bottom of the Trim Video dialog box to cut time from the beginning or end of the video. Click OK to save the changes.

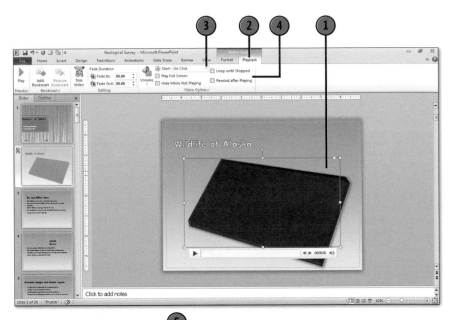

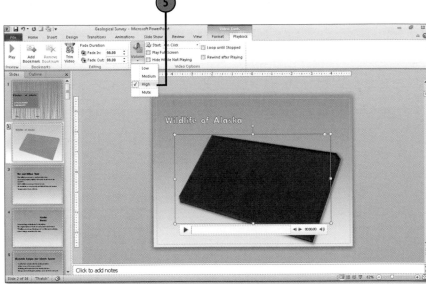

Changing the Slide Background

If you choose a slide theme, a background is automatically applied, but you might want to apply a background of your own choosing. A background can be a solid color, an effect such as a gradient (which makes it appear as though a light source is shining on the background from a certain direction), or even a picture or texture. Backgrounds help make objects and text on the page stand out and add color and interest to your slides.

Change the Background Style

① Display the slide whose background you want to change.

② Click the Design tab.

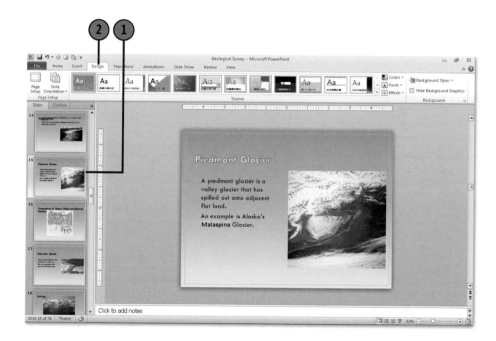

③ Click Background Styles.

④ Click a style to apply it.

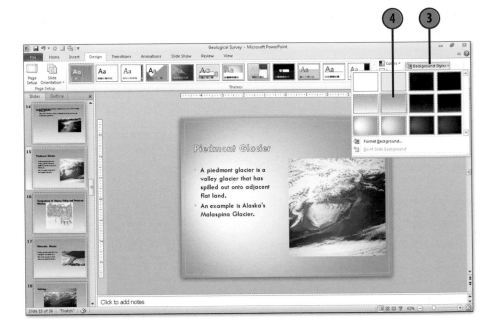

Try This!

You can also customize a background by clicking Format Background at the bottom of the Background gallery. In the Format Background dialog box, choose the type of fill you want to apply (Solid, Gradient, Picture Or Texture, or Pattern), and choose the settings for that type of background.

Tip

You can use the Hide Background Graphics check box in the Format Background dialog box to hide objects you have placed on a slide master. See Section 5, "Working with Slide Masters," starting on page 53, for more about slide masters.

12

Adding Transitions and Animations

Animations in Microsoft PowerPoint are used to transition from one slide to another when you are showing a presentation in slide show mode. They can also be applied to individual objects to cause them to appear on a slide with an effect such as spinning or to appear to grow on the slide.

The transition that occurs when you move from one slide to another in a slide show can vary for each slide change or be applied globally. You can also control the speed of each transition, and you can even add a sound that is played along with the transition effect.

Using a custom animation effect to control how individual objects are displayed on your slides allows you to cause individual bullet points to appear in a timed sequence or one by one as you click your mouse. You can even apply a motion path so that an object enters from a certain direction, moves to one area of the slide, then moves to another, and so forth. New to Microsoft PowerPoint 2010 is Animation Painter, a tool that allows you to copy an animation effect or set of effects from one object to another.

Animations and transitions are a great way to draw attention or add visual interest to your presentation.

Applying a Transition

You can use a gallery of preset animations to apply a transition effect that occurs when a new slide is displayed. These transition effects are divided into categories such as Subtle, Exciting, or Dynamic Content. You can apply a different effect between each pair of slides or one effect that occurs every time a new slide appears.

Apply a Transition Scheme to a Slide

1. If you want a transition to occur when a particular slide appears, display that slide.

2. Click the Transitions tab.

3. Click the More button on the Transitions gallery.

4. Move your mouse pointer over the various effects to see them previewed on your slide.

5. Click a transition effect to apply it to that slide.

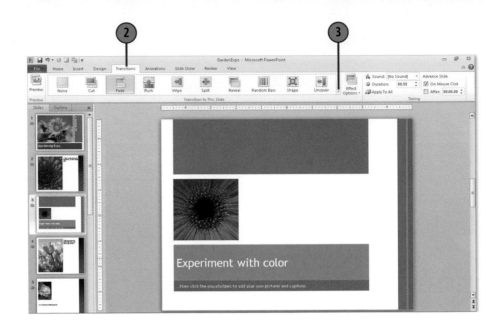

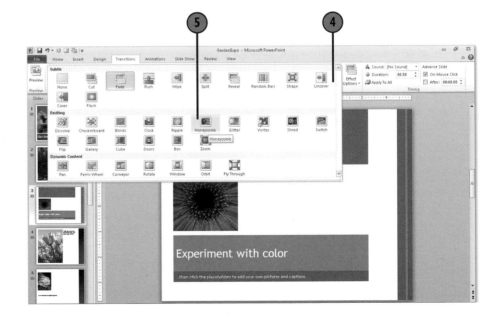

Tip

If you apply a transition to a slide and then decide you don't want to include the transition anymore, select the slide and then click the None option. (This is the first item in the Transition gallery.)

Apply a Transition to All Slides

(1) Click the Transitions tab.

(2) Apply a transition scheme to a slide following the steps in the previous task.

(3) Click the Apply To All button. Stars appear next to all slides in the Slide pane to indicate a transition is applied.

Tip

If you apply a transition to one slide and want to then apply it to all slides, first display that slide in Normal view. Then, on the Animation tab, click Apply To All in the Timing group.

See Also

For more information about adding animations to individual objects on a slide, see "Applying a Custom Animation to an Object" on page 173.

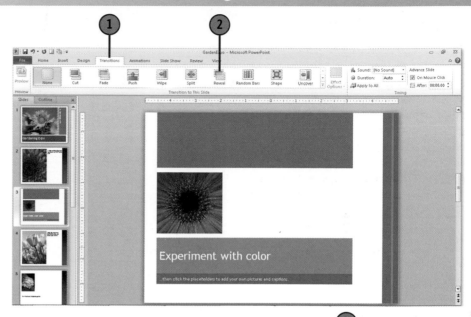

Transition icon

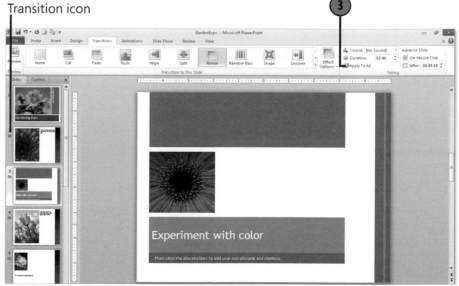

Adding Sound to a Transition

Imagine that you have set up a slide transition so that a new slide appears to fly in from the left side. If you also add a sound effect like a burst of wind, you can add impact to the transition. That's what adding sounds to transitions is all about: catching your audience's attention with a sound that complements the transition effect and the contents of the slide. You can also add sounds to custom animations on individual objects—so, when that clip art of a pile of money appears, why not have a cash register sound happen simultaneously?

Add Sound

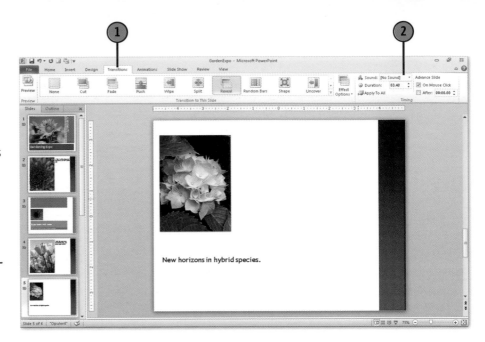

1. Select a slide with a transition applied to it, and click the Transitions tab.

2. Click the Sound list.

See Also

You can apply a sound to an object that has a custom animation applied to it simply by selecting the object before applying the sound. To learn more, see "Modify Animation Settings" on page 174.

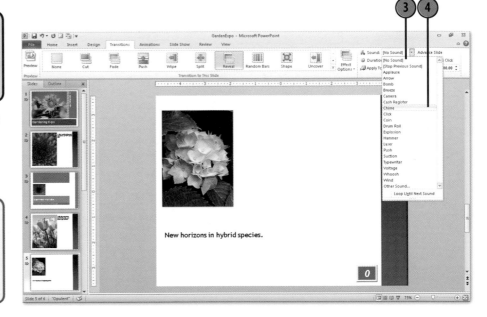

3. Move your pointer over the sounds in the list to preview them.

4. Click a sound to apply it to the current slide.

Try This!

If you want a sound to keep repeating until the next sound is played, click the Loop Until Next Sound option at the bottom of the Sound list. Repeating a sound in this way can be a great effect, but don't let it go on too long, or you'll drive your viewers crazy!

Modifying Transition Speed

Transitions can happen at various speeds. Fast transitions between slides provide a little subconscious shift, but it's so fast that most people don't notice the effect. Transitions that happen slowly, on the other hand, are more noticeable to view-ers, but you run the danger of slowing down your presentation if you overuse them. The ability to control the speed of transitions is useful, but you have to determine which speed best fits each transition and your presentation.

Set the Speed for Transitions

(1) Display a slide that has a transition applied to it.

(2) Click the Transitions tab if necessary.

(3) Use the spinner arrows on the Duration field to display the transition for a longer or shorter time.

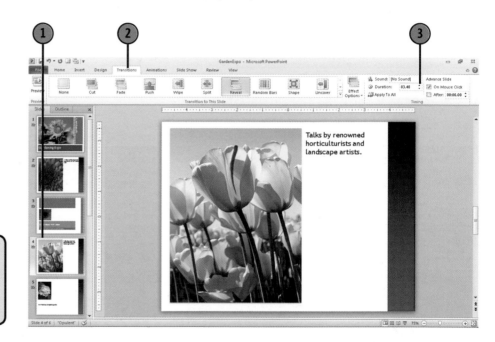

See Also

For information about setting the speed for custom animations applied to individual objects, see "Applying a Custom Animation to an Object" on page 173.

Caution

If you play a sound along with a transition and you set the transition to run fast, the sound occurs quickly, too. In fact, the sound may happen so quickly that it can be hard to tell what the sound is. If you associate a sound like a typewriter, for example, with a fast transition, your viewers might hear a single click of a typewriter key—not enough to know what it is they are hearing!

Tip

To use the transition speed that is applied to the currently selected slide for all the slides in your presentation, click the Apply To All button on the Animations tab.

Choosing How to Advance a Slide

You can advance from slide to slide in a presentation in several ways, such as by clicking your mouse or by waiting for a certain interval of time to pass. The manual approach of clicking your mouse gives you control, but it keeps your hands busy during the presentation. The automatic timed-advance feature is useful when you are showing a slide show on the Web or in an unattended setting, such as a mall kiosk. If you need to have a combination of methods within a presentation, you can make this setting on a slide-by-slide basis by using tools on the Animations tab.

Select a Method to Advance a Slide

① Display a slide with a transition applied to it. Click the Transitions tab.

② If you want to advance slides manually, click the On Mouse Click check box to select it.

③ Clear the On Mouse Click check box to advance the slide according to preset timings.

④ Use the spinner arrows in the After field to set a time interval.

> **See Also**
>
> For more about navigating through a slide show presentation, see "Navigating Through Slides" on page 199.

> **Tip**
>
> You can also use the Right arrow key to advance a presentation, if you have the keyboard handy, or click the Slide tool that appears in Slide Show view and choose Next or Previous from the pop-up menu. Many presentation settings also make a remote control unit available that you can use for forwarding slides.

> **See Also**
>
> You can set up your show so that all slides are advanced using the same method.

Applying a Custom Animation to an Object

You can apply animations to individual objects on your slide, from clip art and pictures to text place-holders. Animations include effects that make an object seem to appear on or disappear from your slide in Slide Show view in some fashion. For example, you might choose to have a heading appear letter by letter or fly onto your slide. The Motion Path category of animations allows you to have the object appear and then move around a path you specify on your slide.

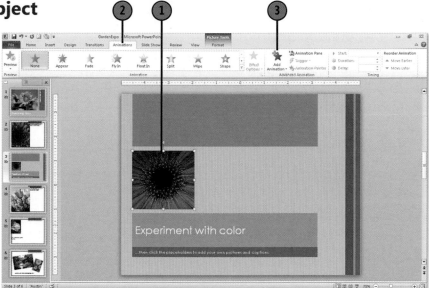

Add an Animation Effect to an Object

1. Click the object to select it.
2. Click the Animations tab.
3. Click Add Animation to display the Animation gallery.
4. Click an effect from the gallery.

Try This!

If you want the same animation applied to all objects of a certain type—for example, to all title objects on slides using the Title And Content layout—apply the custom animation in Slide Master view.

Tip

Don't overdo animations. If they play all the time, your audience can become bored with them. Use them for special emphasis, at the start of a new section of your presentation, or to drive home a key point.

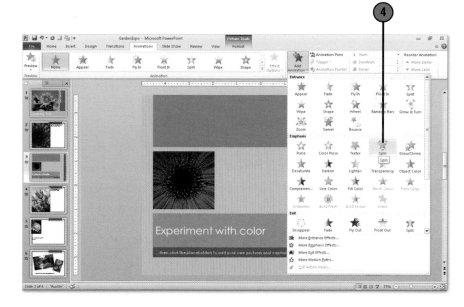

Modify Animation Settings

1 Display a slide that has an object with an animation effect applied to it.

2 Click the Animations tab.

3 Click Animation Pane to display the Animation Pane.

4 Click the arrow at the right side of the animation you want to modify in the list.

5 Click any of the first three settings on this menu to specify whether the effect plays when you click your mouse, along with any previous animation, or after the previous animation.

6 Click the Effect Options command on this menu to open an effect dialog box.

7 On the Effect tab of this dialog box, you can make settings depending on which effect you chose. For example, if your effect shrinks your text, the Font Size field lets you choose the font size to shrink to. If your effect causes the object to spin, the Amount field lets you choose by how many degrees the object should spin.

8 Click the Timing tab, and choose the duration for the effect and whether it should repeat.

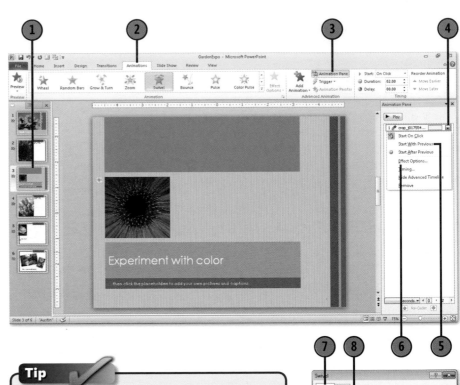

Tip
To remove an animation effect from an object, click the arrow next to it in the list of effects in the Animation Pane and click Remove.

Tip
You can click the arrow at the right of an effect in the list of effects and choose Effect Options from the menu that appears to make all these settings and more in a dialog box. If you select the option of starting an animation after another animation plays, you can use the Timing tab in this dialog box to specify a delay between the two animations.

Reorder Effects

① With the Animation Pane displayed (click the Animation Pane button on the Animations tab), click an effect in the list.

② Click the up arrow in the Re-Order area at the bottom of the pane to move the effect up in the list.

③ Click the down arrow to move the effect down in the list.

④ Repeat steps 1, 2, and 3 to reorganize the list of effects in any way you like.

Tip ✓

If you reorganize slides, remember to check each slide's Start setting. For example, if you want a slide to use a certain entrance effect that relates to the contents of the slide before it, you may want to change the entrance effect to be relevant to its new predecessor when you move that slide .

Tip ✓

You can apply more than one animation to any object—so, you might have a heading shrink its font size, spin around 360 degrees, and then fly off the slide. If you do this, you can use the method described here to reorder the effects applied to that object.

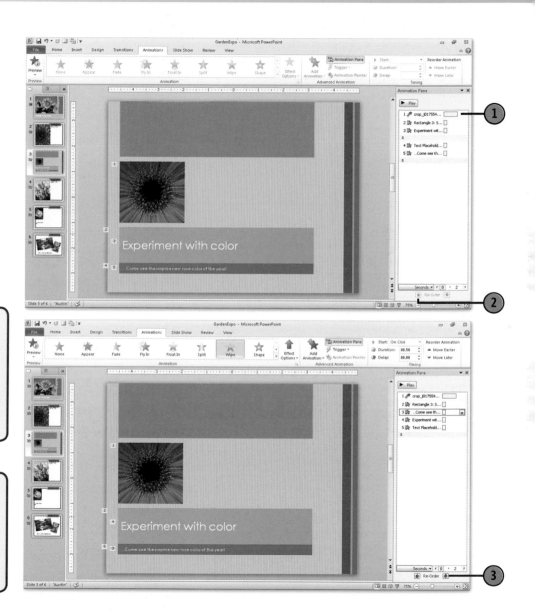

Using Animation Painter

You can apply multiple animation effects to a single object, so the ability to replicate those effects on other objects can be a big time saver. Animation Painter, a feature that's new to PowerPoint 2010, works similarly to Format Painter, which allows you to copy formats such as font and font color from one piece of text to another. Animation Painter, however, copies animation effects from one object to another.

Copy Animations with Animation Painter

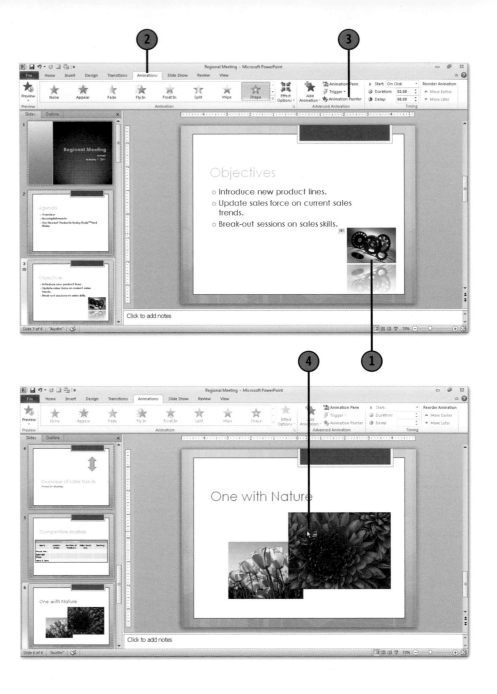

① Click an object that has an animation applied to it to select it.

② Click the Animations tab.

③ Click Animation Painter.

④ Select another object on the same or another slide.

⑤ Click the object to copy all animation effects from the first object to the second.

Tip

Clicking Animation Painter allows you to copy animation effects to one object. If you want to copy the animation effects to more than one other object, double-click the Animation Painter button in step 2. When you finish, press the Esc key to turn off Animation Painter.

Previewing an Animation

PowerPoint offers a couple of options for previewing an animation effect on a slide in Normal view. There is a Preview button on the Animation tab that plays all the effects on a slide, and the Animation Pane offers a Play button to play the individual animations on the animation list. You can also click the Slide Show button in the view buttons to quickly go into Slide Show view.

Preview an Animation

1. With a slide containing animations displayed, click the Animations tab.

2. Click the Preview button to play all animations on the slide.

3. Click Animation Pane.

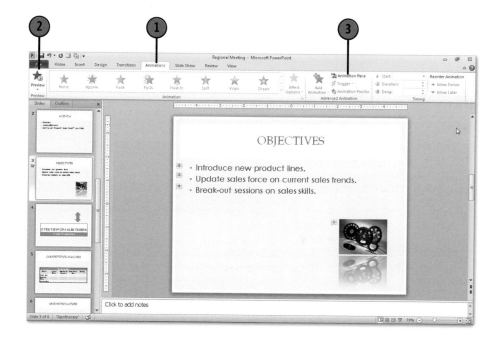

4 Click Play to play the applied animations in sequence.

5 To view the animation in Slide Show view, click the Slide Show button at the bottom right of the PowerPoint window.

6 To stop the preview from running, click the Stop button in the Animation Pane at any time.

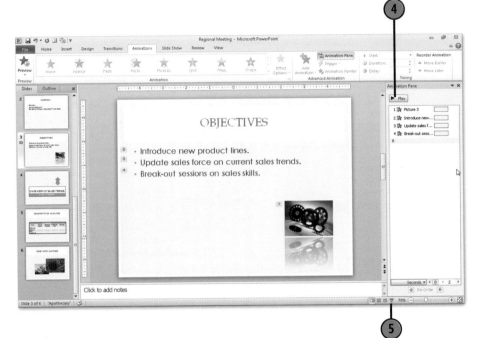

Try This!

If you click the Play button in the Animation pane to preview the animations, a little timer bar appears at the bottom of the list. You can use this to tally up the seconds it takes for all your animations to play.

13

Finalizing Your Slide Show

After you put in all the effort to build a stunning presentation—composing the perfect content and choosing attractive design elements and graphics—you should take the time to proofread it to be sure you haven't made spelling or other errors. Microsoft PowerPoint 2010 provides a spelling checker to help you check your contents, as well as a thesaurus to help you find the perfect word. You can also send the presentation to be reviewed by other people, who can help you spot problems before you give the presentation in front of an audience.

At this point, you should also set up how you want your slide show to run. For example, can you use multiple monitors, and will the presentation run in a continuous loop or just one time from beginning to end? This is also the time to rehearse your presentation to ensure that the slide show runs smoothly. While rehearsing a presentation, you can add a narration and timings that control how long each slide is displayed. These are useful if the presentation runs on its own with no live presenter available.

Reviewing Your Presentation

When you finish adding the last sentence of text and final graphic object to your presentation, you're not quite done. Because your presentation is likely to be displayed on a large screen in front of many people, any error or glitch is likely to undermine the credibility of your message. For that reason, taking the time to check spelling, word choices, and the look of your contents is very important. PowerPoint provides tools to help you check the accuracy of your contents and lets you send your presentation to others to review it to be sure everything looks perfect. You can ask others to make changes or to simply add comments with their suggestions for your review.

Check Spelling

① Open the presentation you want to review. If you want to check the spelling of a single word, select it.

② Click the Review tab.

③ Click Spelling.

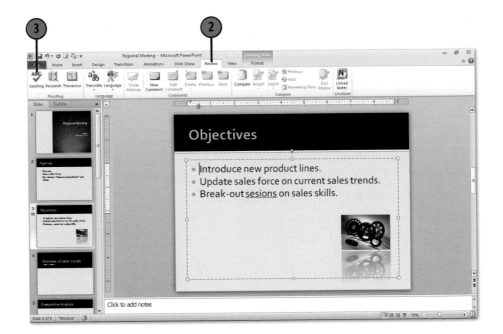

Tip

After working on your presentation for hours, days, or weeks, you are often too close to it to spot problems. In addition to using PowerPoint's spelling checker, be sure to have somebody objective read through the presentation or, if nobody else is available, read each sentence backward yourself to proof it. When we read a sentence forward, we make assumptions about the next word based on context. When we read from the last word to the first, each word and its spelling stand out, and any missing words might be more obvious.

See Also

For information about viewing and moving slides around in your presentation, see "Viewing Slides in the Slide Pane" on page 92 and "Move a Slide" on page 96.

4 Take any of the following actions:

- Click a spelling in the Sugges-tions list, and then click Change or Change All to apply it to the current word or to all instances of the word in your presentation, respectively.

- Enter a new spelling in the Change To box, and then click Change or Change All.

- Click Ignore or Ignore All to disre-gard this instance of the spelling or all instances of it in your presenta-tion, respectively.

- Click Add to add the spelling to the dictionary in PowerPoint.

- Click AutoCorrect if this is a mistake you commonly make and want to add it to the AutoCorrect list to be corrected in the future as you type.

5 When you click one of the previ-ous options, PowerPoint moves to the next word that needs checking. When all errors have been checked, PowerPoint displays a dialog box telling you that the spelling check is complete. Click OK.

Tip

To stop a manual spelling check at any time, just click the Close button in the Spelling dialog box.

Tip

PowerPoint is set up by default to check spelling automatically, which causes wavy colored lines to appear under words that have a questionable spelling. To get rid of those wavy lines on your screen, click the File tab, click Options, and then select Proofing. Select the Hide Spelling Errors check box, and then click OK.

Tip

If you right-click a word that is possibly misspelled, PowerPoint displays alternative spellings or words on the shortcut menu that appears. Just click an entry to make the change.

Use the Thesaurus

1. Display the slide that contains the word you want to check and select that word. If the word you want to check isn't in your presentation, skip this step.

2. Click the Review tab.

3. Click Thesaurus.

4. If you did not select a word prior to clicking the Thesaurus button, enter a word in the Search For box.

5. Click the Start Searching button.

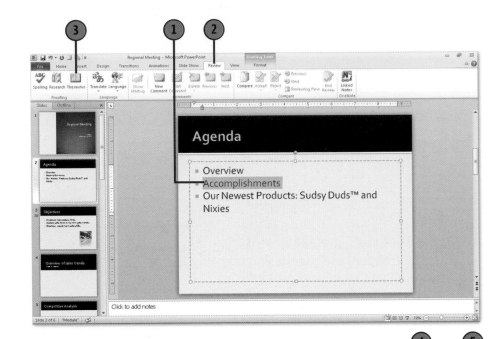

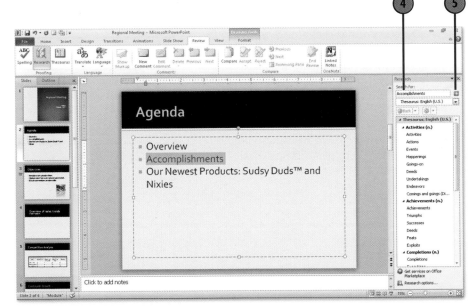

6 Click a word in the list of results to display additional similar words.

7 Click the Back button to move back to a previous list of words.

8 Click the arrow next to a selected word in the Thesaurus and choose Insert to replace the word selected in your presentation or, if no word was selected in step 1, to insert the word in your slide.

9 Click the Close button in the Research task pane.

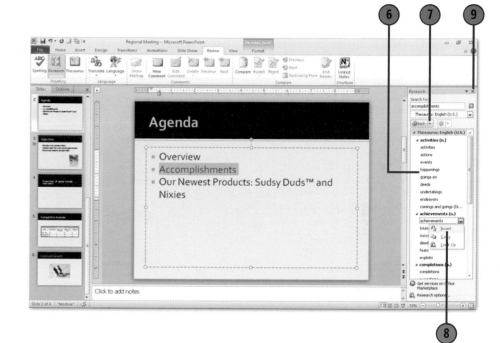

Tip ✓

You can change which resources are searched by clicking the second list in the Search For section of the Research task pane and selecting a different option. These options consist mainly of different language dictionaries and, if you are connected to the Internet, encyclopedias and other research sites.

Add Comments

① Display a slide to which you want to add a comment.

② If you want to attach a comment to a particular object or placeholder, click to select it.

③ Click the Review tab.

④ Click New Comment.

⑤ Type your comment, and then click anywhere outside the comment box.

Try This!

Try using the tools in the Comments group on the Review tab to edit, delete, or cycle through comments in your presentation. To hide all comments from your view, click the Show Markup button.

Tip

Comments do not show up in Slide Show or Slide Sorter view. They are intended mostly for reviewers to provide comments on a presentation as it is being created. If you want to include comments with your presentation, consider adding notes and printing the Notes view for your audience.

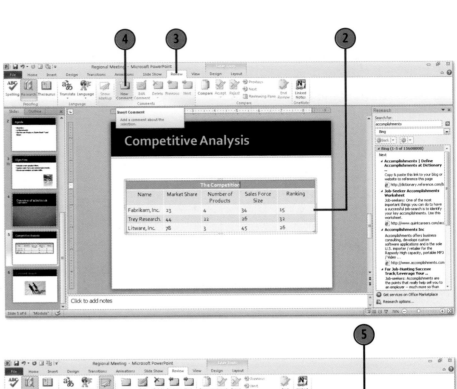

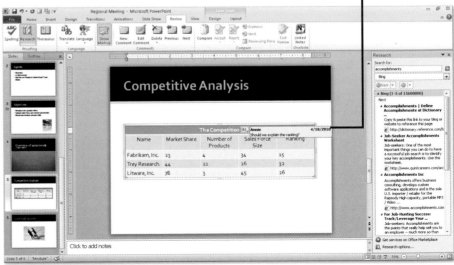

E-Mail a Presentation for Review

1. With the presentation open that you want to send in e-mail, click the File tab.

2. Click Save & Send.

3. Click Send Using E-mail, and then choose whether to send the file as an attachment, a link, or an XPS or PDF document.

4. In the e-mail form that opens in your default e-mail program, type a recipient's e-mail address in the To field.

5. Type a subject in the Subject field.

6. Type the text of any message you want to send in the body of the message.

7. Click Send.

Tip

If you are sending the presentation to somebody who doesn't have PowerPoint available, consider saving the presentation as a PDF or an XPS file. These formats retain most formatting on any Windows computer; however, viewers cannot use reviewing features such as inserting comments and cannot play the show.

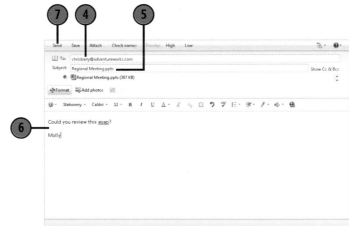

Setting Up a Slide Show

Several variables affect how your slide show runs. For example, you can set up a slide show to be presented by a live speaker or to be browsed by a viewer. You can specify that a show loop continuously or be shown with or without a recorded narration. You can even choose to have only a subset of the slides in the presentation included in a particular slide show. You can set up your show to advance manually when a presenter clicks or automatically according to recorded timings. Finally, you can specify to use more than one monitor. With this feature, the presenter can use one monitor to orchestrate the show while the audience views the presentation on another monitor.

Set the Show Type

1. Click the Slide Show tab.

2. Click Set Up Slide Show.

3. Click one of the three options in the Show type section:

   - Presented By A Speaker displays the slide show in full-screen mode and assumes a live presenter is running the show.

   - Browsed By An Individual is the setting to use if an individual will view the show from a computer or CD. This option runs the presentation in a window rather than full screen.

   - Browsed At A Kiosk provides a self-running, full-screen presentation that might be set up at a kiosk.

4. Click OK to save your settings.

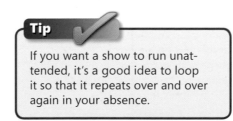

Tip

If you want a show to run unattended, it's a good idea to loop it so that it repeats over and over again in your absence.

Specify Show Options

① Click the Slide Show tab.

② Click Set Up Slide Show.

③ Select any of the three check boxes in the Show Options section:

- Loop Continuously Until 'Esc'. Choose this option if you are running the show unattended and want it to continuously repeat.

- Show Without Narration. If you recorded a narration but now want a live presenter to give the show, select this option.

- Show Without Animation. Because animations might not run smoothly on slower computers, you can turn them off by using this setting.

④ Click the arrow on the Pen Color list and choose an ink color from the drop-down palette for annotations you can make while running a show.

⑤ Click OK to save your settings.

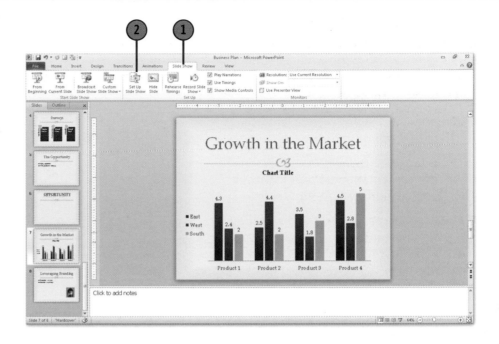

See Also

For information about working with the pen to make annotations during a presentation, see "Make Annotations on Slides" on page 203.

Tip

You can choose additional colors for the pen by clicking More Colors at the bottom of the drop-down palette. This displays the Colors dialog box, where you can select a standard or custom color to apply. You can also use your mouse as a laser pointer during a slide show by holding down Ctrl and pressing the left mouse button. Set the laser pointer color using the Laser Pointer Color drop-down palette in the Set Up Show dialog box.

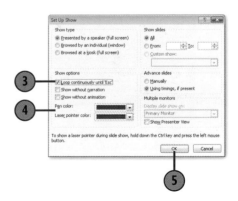

Specify Which Slides to Include

(1) Click the Slide Show tab.

(2) Click Set Up Slide Show.

(3) In the Show Slides section, choose one of three options:

- Choose All to include all slides in the presentation (except for slides you've hidden).

- Enter beginning and ending slide numbers in the From and To boxes to show a range of slides.

- Click Custom Show to pick and choose any number or range of slides you want to present. This feature enables you to present different versions of your show to different audiences.

(4) Click OK to save your settings.

See Also

For information about working with custom shows, see "Creating Custom Shows" on page 229.

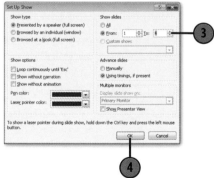

Try This!

If you have a large slide show and find it's running slowly on the presenting computer, don't shorten your show. Instead, you can modify your monitor's resolution in Windows Control Panel by using the Adjust Screen Resolution link. Your slides run faster at a lower resolution, such as 600×800, although the image quality is grainier.

Set Up How to Advance Slides

① Click the Slide Show tab.

② Click Set Up Slide Show.

③ Click an option for how to advance slides:

- Manually requires you to click a mouse, press an arrow key, or use the navigation tools in Slide Show view.

- Using Timings, If Present moves the slides forward automatically based on the timings you save when you rehearse the show and save timings.

④ Click OK to save your settings.

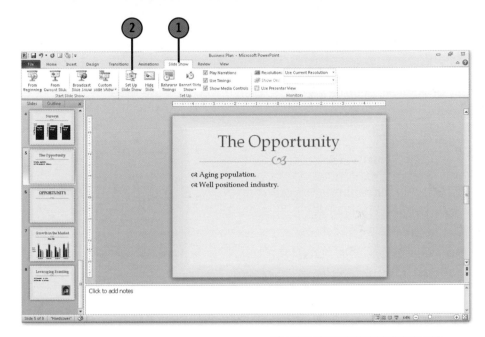

The Opportunity

ca Aging population.
ca Well positioned industry.

Tip

The Show Presenter View option in the Set Up Show dialog box can come in handy if you have a system with multiple monitors. Select it if you want to control the show from one screen—your laptop, for instance—but use another screen to display the presentation to your viewers. By using the Show Presenter View option on your screen, you can navigate the slide show, and your actions are invisible to your viewers. For example, you can use thumbnails of your slides to build a custom presentation, reordering slides to offer a recap of key ideas on the fly.

See Also

For more information about how to move from slide to slide in a presentation, see "Navigating Through Slides" on page 199.

Try This!

When you record a narration, you are offered the option of saving timings as well. If you do, those timings can be used to advance slides based on when the narration for each slide is complete. The Slide Show tab includes a Use Timings check box that you can select to override narration timings.

Rehearsing Your Presentation

It's very important that you prepare for your presentation. Rehearsing has several benefits. First, during rehearsal you can save timings that can be used to advance your slides automatically or you can record a narration. Even if you don't use those timings to navigate your presentation, they help you anticipate whether your presentation runs under or over the allotted time. In addition, rehearsing helps you spot problems in running your presentation, such as animations that take a long time to play or type that is hard to read.

Add a Narration

① Attach a microphone to your computer if one is not built in.

② Click the Slide Show tab.

③ Click the arrow on the Record Slide Show button, and choose to record from the beginning or from the currently displayed slide.

④ In the dialog box that appears, choose to record narrations and laser pointers, and then click the Start Recording button.

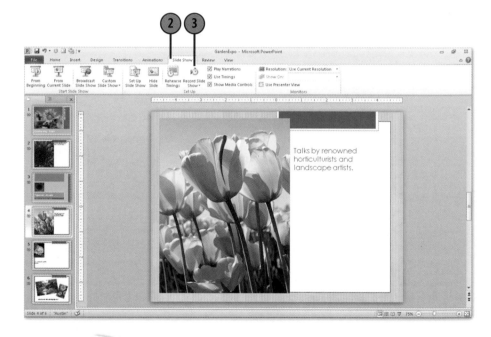

Tip

Your sound quality is better if you have a more sensitive microphone. It might be worth spending a bit more for a better microphone headset to provide quality recording. Typically, an outlet for plugging in a microphone or a headset is on the back or front of your computer, and no other special hardware is required.

Try This!

You can clear timings you recorded previously by clicking the Record Slide Show button and choosing Clear. In the menu that appears, you can clear timings or narrations on the current slide or for all slides

5 The presentation begins, and the Recording dialog box appears in the upper-left corner. Navigate through the presentation reading your narration into your microphone.

6 To stop recording at any point, click the Close button on the Recording dialog box.

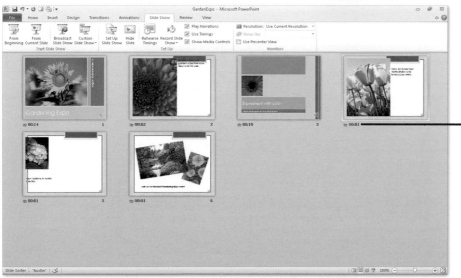

When you reach the end of the presentation, the slide show closes, and Slide Sorter view is displayed with timings displayed beneath each slide.

Save Timings

① Click the Slide Show tab.

② Click Rehearse Timings.

③ Navigate through your slide show, displaying each slide for the approximate length of time you want to show it and discuss its contents.

④ When the slide show is done, in the dialog box that displays the total time for the show, click Yes to keep the settings or No to discard them.

⑤ Click the Slide Sorter view button and note that saved timings appear beneath slides.

See Also

For more information about running your slide show, see the tasks "Navigating Through Slides" on page 199 and "End a Show" on page 198.

Tip

If you add to or change the content of your presentation in any way, you might want to change the saved timings. To save new timings, simply run the Rehearse Timings feature again and save the timings. Only one set of timings can be saved with your slides.

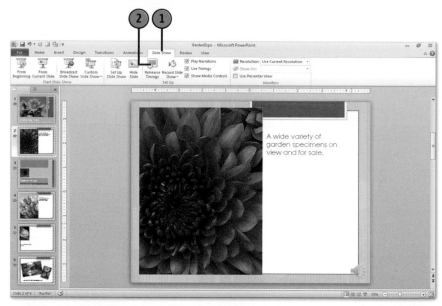

Taking a Presentation with You

Most of the time, you don't give a presentation where you designed it. Instead, you take it on the road, whether the locale is a meeting room two doors down or in another state or country. To do this, you save a presentation to media such as a CD. When you publish your presentation to media in this way, you can also add the PowerPoint Viewer so that you can run the presentation on a computer that doesn't have PowerPoint installed.

Save a Presentation to CD

1. Insert a CD or DVD in your computer's CD/DVD drive.

2. Click the File tab.

3. Click Save & Send.

4. Click Package Presentation For CD.

5. Click Package For CD in the pane that appears.

6. In the Package For CD dialog box, enter a name for the CD.

7. If you want to add more files, such as files you need for background information, click Add and select them. (Note that you will be prompted to include linked files when you initiate the copying process.)

8. Click Copy To CD.

9. Click Yes in the message box that appears asking whether you want to include linked files.

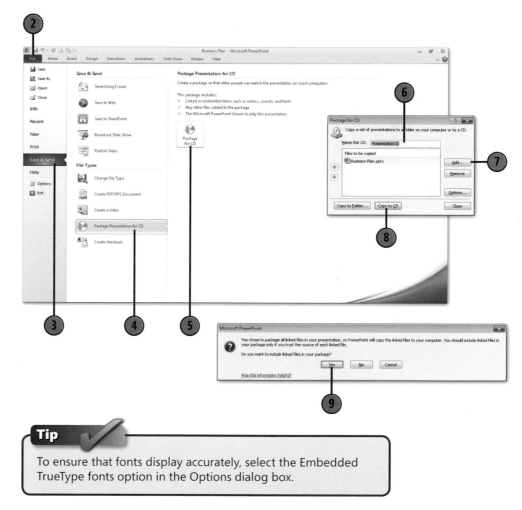

Tip

To ensure that fonts display accurately, select the Embedded TrueType fonts option in the Options dialog box.

14

Running a Presentation

After you build your slides, set up your slide show, rehearse your presentation, and save it to a CD or USB stick, the time comes to present your slide show to an audience. If the show is set up to be given by a live presenter, the presenter must know how to run the show, navigate between slides, annotate slides, and other tasks. (For more about settings for live presentations, see Section 13, "Finalizing Your Slide Show," starting on page 179.)

Microsoft PowerPoint 2010 offers a few different ways to move around a presentation and also a set of annotation tools that allows you to make notes as you present. If your presentation sparks interesting ideas, action items, or questions you need to follow up on, you can use the annotation tools to jot notes and save those annotations with your presentation. You can also switch to another program or even go online while presenting to display other kinds of documents and content.

Knowing how to use these tools can make the difference between a smooth presentation and an awkward viewing and presenting experience.

Starting and Ending a Slide Show

Starting a slide show simply involves displaying Slide Show view. This view shows your slides in full-screen mode (unless you set up your show to be browsed by an individual, in which case your slides appear with a scroll bar around them). In Slide Show view, there are no speaker's notes or tool tabs in evidence, although a set of presentation tools appears in the bottom-right corner of the screen when you move your mouse pointer over them. You learn more about these tools in the following two tasks.

Start a Show

1. If you are using some form of LCD or other display equipment, connect it to your computer and turn it on.

2. Open the presentation you want to present.

3. If you want to start the show from the first slide, display it.

4. Click the Slide Show icon.

See Also

For information about switching between views in PowerPoint, see "Running a Presentation in Slide Show View" on page 47.

The slide show begins.

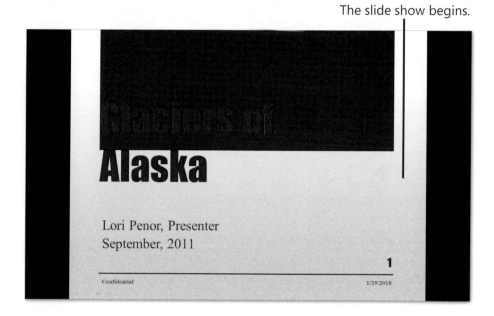

End a Show

① With a presentation running in Slide Show view, do one of the following:

- Press the Esc key.

- Click the Slide Show Menu icon, and choose End Show.

- Click Break.

- Press the hyphen key [-].

- Navigate to the last slide in the presentation, and press the Right arrow key. A black screen appears with a message that instructs you to click your mouse to end the show.

Tip

If you want to temporarily remove your presentation from the screen, you don't have to exit the show. Instead, you can click the Slide Show Menu icon, choose Screen, and then choose the Black Screen or White Screen command. This step is useful if you pause for a discussion and don't want people to be distracted by the words and images on the screen.

Tip

Did you forget how to jump to another slide or some other handy navigation shortcut? Don't worry. Click the Slide Show Menu icon and choose Help. A Slide Show Help window appears listing common keyboard commands. This list includes some very useful shortcuts; for example, to go to a black screen, you can simply type "b".

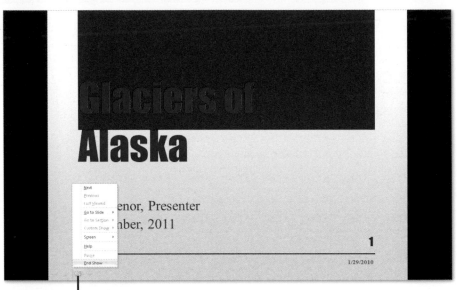

Slide Show Menu icon

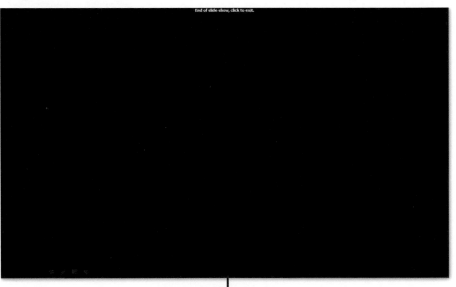

Screen after the last slide

Navigating Through Slides

There are times when you need to move back to a previous slide to reinforce a point or jump ahead when somebody anticipates a topic through a question or comment. Here are a few different methods you can use to navigate from slide to slide.

Move to Next and Previous Slide

① Click the Slide Show icon to display Slide Show view.

② Use any of these methods to move to the next or previous slide:

- Press the Right arrow key for the next slide, or the Left arrow key for the previous slide.

- Click your mouse button to get to the next slide.

- Click the Next or Previous arrow.

- Click the Slide Show Menu icon, and choose Next or Previous.

- Press Spacebar for the next slide, or Backspace for the previous slide.

- Press the Page Up key for the next slide, or the Page Down key for the previous slide.

- Type "N" to go to the next slide, or "P" to go to the previous slide.

Try This!

You can access the Slide Show menu by right-clicking anywhere on your screen while running a slide show. Then click Next or Previous to move forward or backward in your presentation.

Features of Scouring

- Scouring causes striations.
- Abrasion can polish the surface of some rock types.
- Scouring also produces a fine clay-sized sediment transported away from the glacier by meltwater.
- Glacial meltwater can have a light, cloudy appearance, and is called glacial milk.

Next arrow
Slide Show Menu icon

An East Coast US 'island' is actually a terminal moraine. Is it:

a) Rhode Island
b) Long Island
c) Roanoke Island
d) Brunswick Islands

Name the East Coast "Island"

Previous arrow

Go to a Particular Slide

① Click the Slide Show icon to display Slide Show view.

② Use any of these methods to move to any slide in the presentation:

- Click the Slide Show Menu icon, choose Go To Slide, and then click the title of the slide you want to go to.

- Press the slide number on your keyboard, and press Enter.

- Press Ctrl+S. The All Slides dialog box appears showing a list of all slide titles. Click a title, and then click Go To.

Slide Show Menu icon

The All Slides dialog box

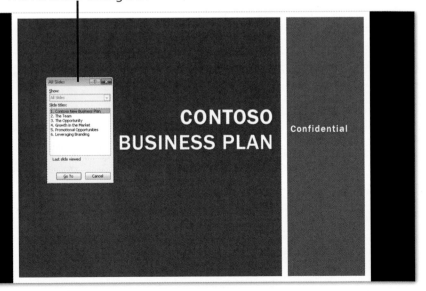

Tip

You can use the Home and End keys on your keyboard to move to the first or last slide in your presentation. You can also hold down both the right and left mouse buttons for a few seconds to jump to the last or first slide.

Try This!

You can decide you want to display a hidden slide. When you get to the slide before the hidden one, press H, and PowerPoint goes ahead and shows the hidden slide. To return to the last slide you had displayed, click the Slide Show Menu icon, and choose Last Viewed from the menu that appears.

Start a Custom Show

1 Open a presentation that contains a custom show.

2 Click the Slide Show tab.

3 Click Custom Slide Show.

4 In the Custom Shows dialog box that appears, click the custom show title. PowerPoint displays the show in Slide Show view.

Try This!

If you create a large presentation, create summary slides that introduce each major section of the show. Then create a custom show that consists of those summary slides. You can go to that custom show at the end of the larger show to review the major topics.

See Also

For information about working with custom shows, see "Creating Custom Shows" on page 229.

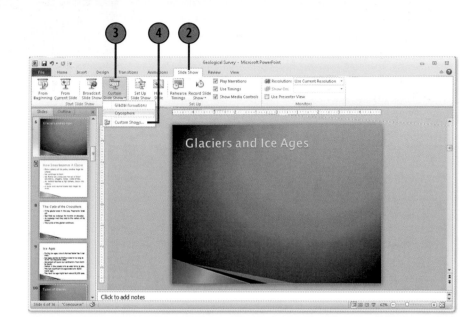

Custom Shows
dialog box

Working with the Pen and Annotations

A tool called a *pen* allows you to use a technology that Microsoft calls ink to write on your slides when running your presentation in Slide Show view. The Pen tool allows you to select different pen types, such as ballpoint, felt tip, and highlighter, and to change the ink color. You can use the pen to write on slides and then use an eraser tool to remove the writing, or you can use a command to remove all ink markings on a slide. At the end of your presentation, you are offered the option of saving your ink annotations or discarding them.

Choose a Pen Style and Color

① Click the Slide Show view icon to begin your presentation.

② Click the Pen button.

③ Click a pen style to select it.

④ Click the Pen button again, and this time click Ink Color.

⑤ Click a color in the palette that appears.

Try This!

You can also use the Pen menu to make changes to the arrow pointer that appears when the pen isn't activated. Click the Pen button, and then click Arrow to return to the arrow pointer after using the pen; open the menu again, click Arrow Options, and choose Automatic, Visible, or Hidden to specify whether the arrow pointer is visible only when you move the mouse or all the time or if it should be invisible.

Make Annotations on Slides

(1) With a slide displayed in Slide Show view, click the Pen button and choose a pen style.

(2) Click the screen, and then draw or write wherever you want to using your mouse. If you chose the highlighter pen style, drag over the object or text you want to highlight.

(3) To turn off the pen, click the Pen button, and choose Arrow.

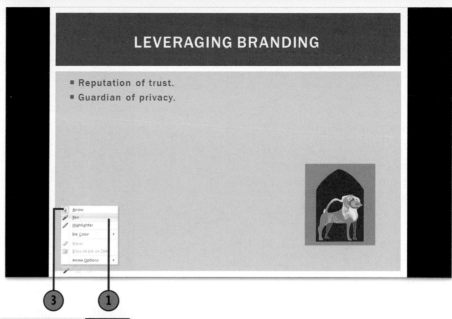

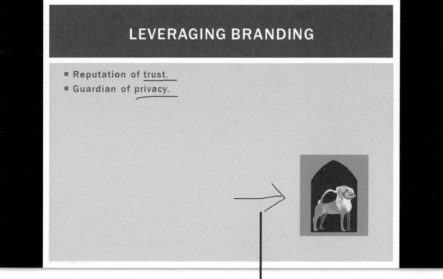

See Also

If you choose a pen color other than the default to write on a slide, be aware that when you move to another slide the default pen color takes over again. For more about choosing a default pen color, see "Specify Show Options" on page 187.

Erase Annotations on Slides

1 Click the Pen button.

2 Choose Eraser.

3 Move the mouse pointer over the annotation you want to remove.

4 To erase all annotations on a slide, click the Pen button, and choose Erase All Ink On Slide.

Tip

Here are a few shortcuts for turning these tools on and off. To quickly change from the arrow pointer to the Pen tool, press Ctrl+P. To change from the arrow pointer to the Eraser tool, press Ctrl+E. To return to the arrow, press Ctrl+A. To turn off the Pen or Eraser tool, you can simply press Esc on your keyboard.

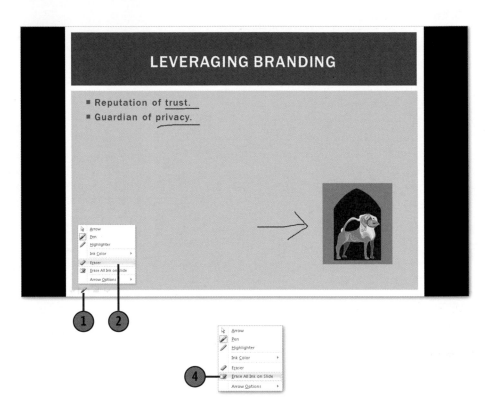

Save Annotations

① Navigate to the end of a presentation in which you've made annotations.

② When you click to end the show, a dialog box appears.

③ Click Keep to save your annotations and Discard if you don't want to save them.

④ Saved annotations appear on the slides in Normal view.

Tip

After you save an annotation, even if you go back to Slide Show view, you can't use the Eraser tool to erase it. That's because ink annotations are objects that can be resized, rotated, moved, and so on, just like any other object. To remove them from your presentation in Normal view, you can simply click one and press Delete.

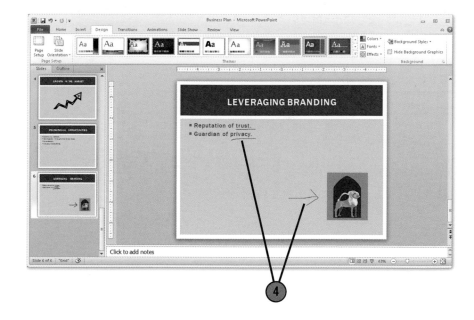

Switching to Another Program

There are many reasons to switch to another program installed on your computer while you are running a PowerPoint presentation. You might want to demo a software system or run a new product demo in a movie program, or you might want to go to the Internet and browse for information to answer a question. Although you can place links in your presentation that open documents in other programs, if you prefer to open the programs themselves to work in them, you can do so easily.

Switch to Another Program

① With a slide show running and the program you want to switch to open, click the Slide Show Menu icon and choose Screen.

② Click Switch Programs.

③ Click the program name on the Windows taskbar that appears.

④ When you're done working in the program, simply click the Close or Minimize button.

Tip

If you'd rather place a hyperlink to a particular document, including a Web page, in your presentation, use the Hyperlink command on the Insert menu. Then click the link while running your slide show and the document or Web page opens.

Cirque Glacier

▸ Cirque glaciers are the smallest of glaciers.
▸ They form in amphitheater–like bowls.
▸ Cirques are confined to the basins they form in.

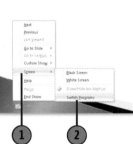

① ②

Paths of Least Resistance

▸ Glaciers generally flow along a path of least resistance.
   s they connect with other glaciers
   ecting valleys.
   er grows in size.

③

See Also

For more information about action buttons that you can use to jump to other documents and programs, see "Drawing Shapes and Text Boxes" on page 139.

15

Printing a Presentation

You might choose to print your presentation for any number of reasons. Perhaps you want others to review it to help you correct or edit it before you present your slide show. Or you might want to print audience handouts or a copy for yourself to refer to while presenting the show. You might also want to preserve a printout of the outline of your contents for your files or to use as the basis for another document.

Whatever your reason for printing your presentation, Microsoft PowerPoint 2010 provides tools to help you preview your printed document, add headers or footers, and choose printing options such as page orientation.

When you print your slides, you can choose how many slides to print on a page. You can print audience handouts that include several slides on a page and leave space for taking notes. You can also print one slide per page with your speaker notes included. Finally, you can print the Outline view of a presentation, which includes only the outline text.

Inserting Headers and Footers

Before you print slides, you might want to include information such as slide number, the date and time the presentation is printed, or the name of the author of the presentation. To do so, you use the Header and Footer feature. You can insert separate headers and footers on slides and on notes and handouts. You can also choose to omit header and footer text on the title slide of a presentation.

Insert Headers or Footers

① Click the Insert tab.

② Click Header & Footer.

Tip

All items inserted using the Slide tab of the Header And Footer dialog box are inserted as footers, but you can drag footers to place them anywhere on an individual slide in Normal view or on the slide master. The Notes And Handouts tab uses both header and footer placeholders, and again, you can move those placeholders around in the Notes Page view or handout master.

See Also

For information about working with footer placeholders using the slide master feature, see "Insert Footer Information" on page 56.

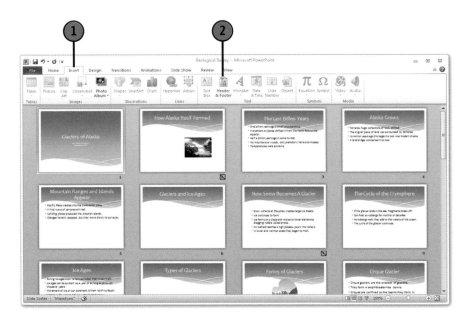

3 Click either the Slide or Notes And Handouts tab, depending on where you want to set headers and footers.

4 Click the Date And Time check box to include a date and/or time, and then choose either of these options:

- Update Automatically, to include the current date and/or time. If you choose this option, use the drop-down lists to select a date/time format, language, and calendar type. The date is updated every time you open the slide show.

- Fixed, to include a date you specify by typing it in.

5 Click the Slide Number check box to include the number of each slide.

6 Click the Footer check box, and then enter text to appear in the footer.

7 If you are working with the Slide tab, you can select the Don't Show On Title Slide check box to omit the footer information from any slide with a Title Slide layout.

8 Click Apply To All to apply the settings to all slides. On the Slide tab, you have the option to click Apply if you want to apply the settings only to the current slide.

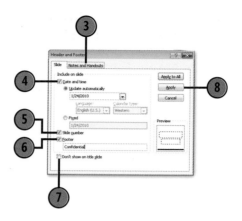

Placeholders now appear on slides.

Using Print Preview

In PowerPoint 2010, Print Preview has been included as part of the print options displayed when you choose Print from the File menu. It's very useful for previewing documents—including handouts, Outline view, and notes pages—before you print them. Print Preview also offers a zoom slider that allows you to view your previews at various sizes.

Display Print Preview

① Click File.

② Click Print. The preview appears to the right of the print options.

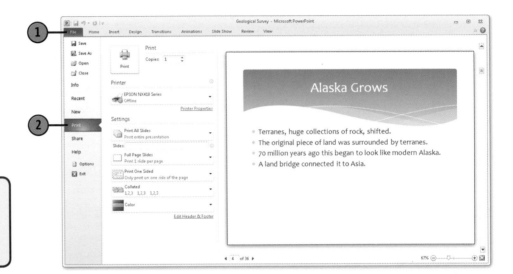

Tip

The zoom slider in the bottom-right corner of the PowerPoint window works in Print Preview as well. Use it to zoom in on and out of your preview to review the contents.

See Also

You can add a Print Preview icon to the Quick Access Toolbar if you want to open Print Preview with a single click. For more information about setting up the Quick Access Toolbar, see "Customizing the Quick Access Toolbar" on page 29.

Navigate Print Preview

① Drag the scroll bar to move to any slide in the presentation.

② Click above or below the scroll bar to move forward or backward one slide or page at a time.

③ Click the Next Page or Previous Page button to move forward or backward one slide or page at a time.

④ Enter a number in the current page indicator in the bottom-left corner of the preview pane and press Enter to display that slide.

⑤ Click Zoom To Page to adjust the size of the slide to fill the window.

Tip

The Zoom dialog box lets you choose a percentage in which to display a slide. You can double-click the percentage number on the zoom slider to quickly display the Zoom dialog box in Print Preview.

Establishing Printer Settings and Printing

The PowerPoint print options include some settings that are probably familiar to you from word processor or spreadsheet programs and some that are specific to PowerPoint. For example, you can choose to print slides, the presentation outline, handouts, or notes pages. You can also choose how many slides to include on a single page if you are printing slides, handouts, or notes. If you haven't used a Microsoft Office 2010 product before, however, you'll find that print options are accessed a bit differently than in previous versions.

Choose a Printer and Paper Options

1. On the File menu, click Print.

2. Choose a printer from the Printer drop-down list.

3. Click Printer Properties. (The Properties dialog box shows settings specific to your printer model.)

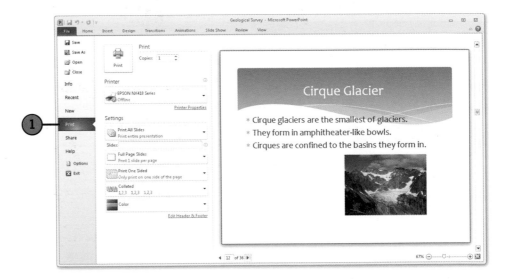

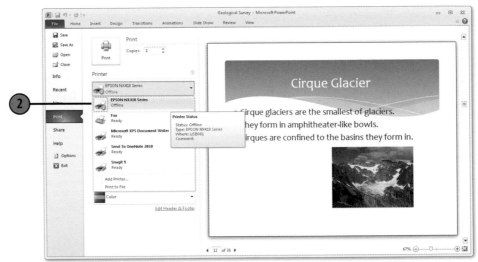

4 Set options available for your printer, such as changing the paper size or orientation.

5 Click OK to save the settings and return to the Print Settings window. At this point, you can continue to change the settings as described in the next three tasks or click Print to print your presentation.

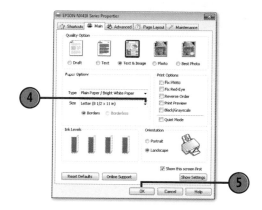

Tip

Different printers offer different property options. For example, if you have a color printer, you can choose to print in color or grayscale. You might be able to select media type, such as printing to glossy paper or to transparencies for overhead projection. Take a look at your Printer Properties dialog box to see what settings are available to you.

Tip

If you want the same printer to be the default option every time you print, go to the Windows Control Panel (Start, Control Panel, and then click the printers link), right-click a printer, and choose Set As Default Printer. You can still change the printer when you print an individual file, but that setting applies only to the document you are printing.

Choose Which Slides to Print

① Open Print settings from the File menu (see previous task).

② Click Print What and choose any of the following options:

- Print All Slides to print all the slides in the presentation.

- Print Current Slide to print only the currently displayed slide.

- Print Selection to print whatever contents you select prior to opening the Print settings. Selecting this option limits your navigation in Print Preview to just the selected slides.

- Custom Range to print a range or selection of slides. Enter slide numbers or a range (2, 15, or 3–15, for example).

③ Click Print to print the specified slides.

Tip

If you want to prepare a printed outline of your presentation in Microsoft Word rather than in PowerPoint, you can cut the outline from the PowerPoint Outline pane, paste it into Word, and then prepare the outline for printing from Word's Print options.

Choose the Format to Print

1. Open Print settings from the File menu.

2. Under Settings, choose the type of output to print.

3. Choose the Print Layout. If you select Handouts, click the number of slides per page you want and select whether to add a frame by selecting Frame Slides.

4. Choose a horizontal option in the Handouts area to print pages with multiple slides progressing from right to left across the page. Click a vertical option to have slides progress down the page along the left margin and then move to the top of the right side of the page in a second column.

5. Click Print.

See Also

For more information about working with handouts and notes layouts, see "Working with Handout and Notes Masters" on page 63.

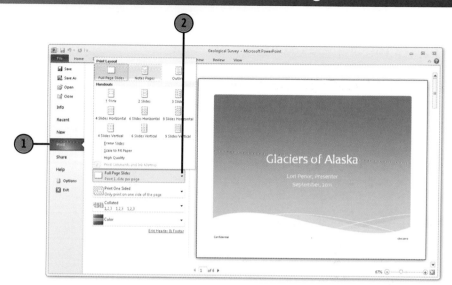

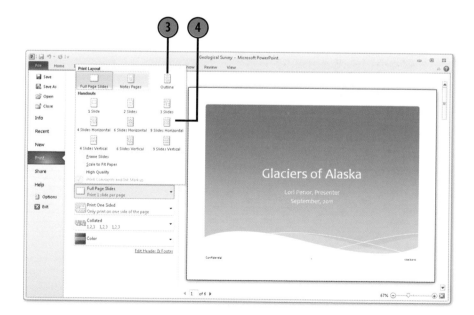

Specify the Number of Copies to Print

1 Open Print settings from the File menu.

2 In the Copies box, click the spinner arrows up or down until the number of copies you want to print appears.

3 Click Collated to collate the pages of multiple copies. Use the Print Sides button to print on one or both sides of the paper.

4 Click Print.

If you have to print a lot of copies and want to save pages, consider modifying the number of slides per page that you print for handouts or notes pages. For more information about this setting, see "Choose the Format to Print" on page 215.

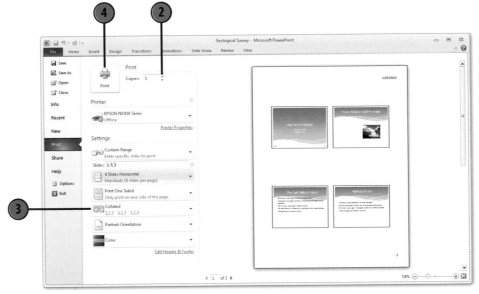

16

Sharing a Presentation on the Web

The ability to publish a presentation to the Internet as a Web document allows you to share your ideas with anybody, any time. You can, for example, publish your presentation as a follow up to giving it in person so that your audience can review or print the content for themselves at their leisure. You might also publish a presentation to the Web for others to review and suggest changes before you present it.

You can ave a presentation to the Web by using a Windows Live ID and placing the presentation in either a public or a private folder.

You can also save a file in PDF format, which is easily viewed by anybody using the free Adobe Reader. This step is a handy way to share the file with those who don't have Microsoft PowerPoint or to view it on the Web.

Finally, you can broadcast your presentation to people in a remote location using a Windows Live account on the Internet. People can view your presentation in their browsers or create a video version of your presentation.

Saving a Presentation to the Web

To save a presentation to the Web, you need a Windows Live ID. The presentation is then saved to Windows Live as a free service to PowerPoint users. This is very handy for sharing the presentation online.

Save to the Web

① Click the File tab.

② Click Send & Save, and then click Save To Web.

③ Click the Sign In button to sign in to your Windows Live account, and then enter your user name and password in the dialog box that appears.

④ Click a folder to save the presentation to.

⑤ Click Save As.

Tip

Go to *www.home.live.com*, and click the Sign Up button. A Windows Live account from Microsoft is free and provides you with an e-mail account as well as access to Windows Live SkyDrive, the free online storage feature that enables you to post and share presentations online.

6 In the Save As dialog box, modify the file name if you want to, and then click Save.

7 To access your presentation on the Web, go to the Windows Live home page, click More, and then click SkyDrive on the menu that appears. SkyDrive opens and displays your folders.

8 Click a folder to open it, and then click the presentation you want to view.

9 To run the presentation, click the preview box on the left side of the screen. The presentation opens in a new window.

Tip

Versions of PowerPoint prior to 2007 contained a Web toolbar, but that feature is missing in PowerPoint 2010. Instead, you can add Web tools to the Quick Access Toolbar. (See Section 3, "Getting Started with PowerPoint 2010," starting on page 21, for more about this toolbar.) The tools you can place on the toolbar include the Web Options button and Web Page Preview button.

Tip

You can share the presentation with others by using Live Messenger. (When you sign up for Windows Live, you also get a free Live Messenger account.) Just right-click a presentation displayed in step 9, choose Share With Live Messenger, and follow the instructions.

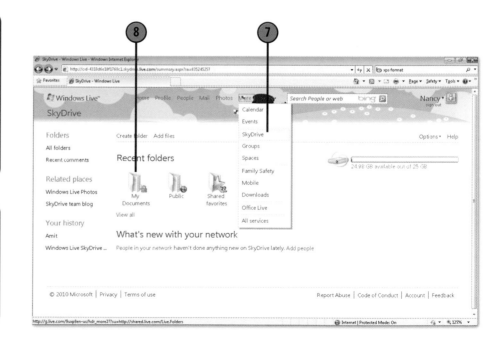

Share a Web Presentation

1. Follow the steps in the previous task to save your presentation to the Public folder.

2. Go to Windows Live, open SkyDrive, and then double-click the Public folder to open it.

3. Click More, and then click Share.

4. Click the E-Mail A Link To This Item link.

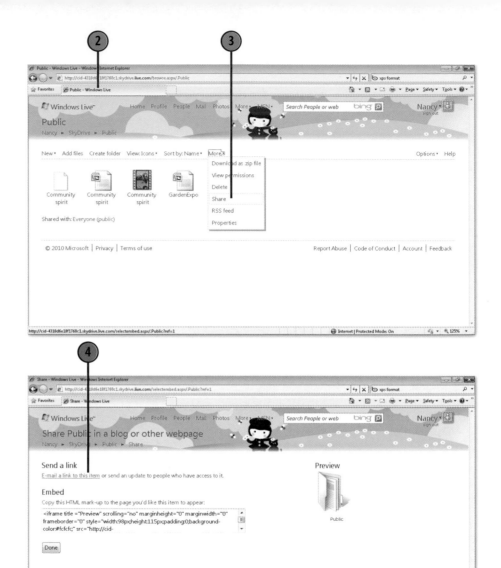

⑤ Enter an e-mail address in the To field.

⑥ Enter a message if you like, and then click the Send button. A link to your presentation is sent via e-mail.

See Also

For information about saving your presentation to the default PowerPoint format, see "Save a Presentation" on page 49.

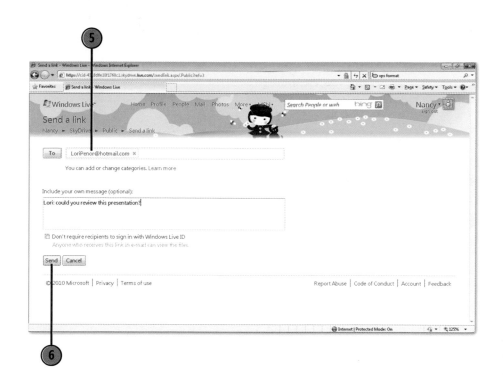

Saving as a PDF File

An easy format to use to share a presentation online is PDF, or Portable Document Format. Anybody with Adobe Acrobat or the free Adobe Reader can view the presentation as the pages of a document. However, they cannot edit the file.

Save a Presentation as a PDF File

1 Choose Save & Send from the File menu.

2 Click Create PDF/XPS Document, and then click the Create PDF/XPS button that appears.

3 In the Publish As PDF Or XPS dialog box, type a name for the document of up to 255 characters. You cannot use the characters * : < > | " \ or /.

4 Be sure that the Save As Type list shows the PDF format, and then click Publish. The PDF document is displayed in an Adobe Reader window.

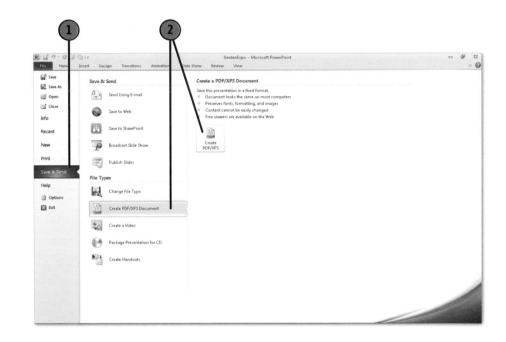

Tip

XPS is an electronic paper document developed by Microsoft that is also used to share your presentation with others who don't have PowerPoint. Also, if you save a file as a PowerPoint Show, the PowerPoint Viewer is built in, allowing those without PowerPoint to view the show.

Try This!

For a free copy of Adobe Reader, go to http://get.adobe.com/reader/, and click the Download button.

Tip

You can also send PDF files using e-mail simply by attaching them to your e-mail message.

Broadcasting a Presentation

When you broadcast a presentation you make it available as a live presentation that others can view using their Web browsers. The process is simple, doesn't require you to have your own site to host the presentation, and is an excellent way to give a live presentation to remote viewers.

Start a Broadcast

1. Click the File tab.

2. Click Save & Send.

3. Click the Broadcast Slide Show link, and then click the Broadcast Slide Show button that appears.

4. In the Broadcast Slide Show dialog box, click the Start Broadcast button. Enter your user ID and password if requested, and click OK.

5. Click the Start Broadcast button to use the default PowerPoint Broadcast Service.

6. Click Copy Link to copy the Web address, and then paste it into an e-mail invitation yourself, or click the Send In Email link to simply open an e-mail message and send the link.

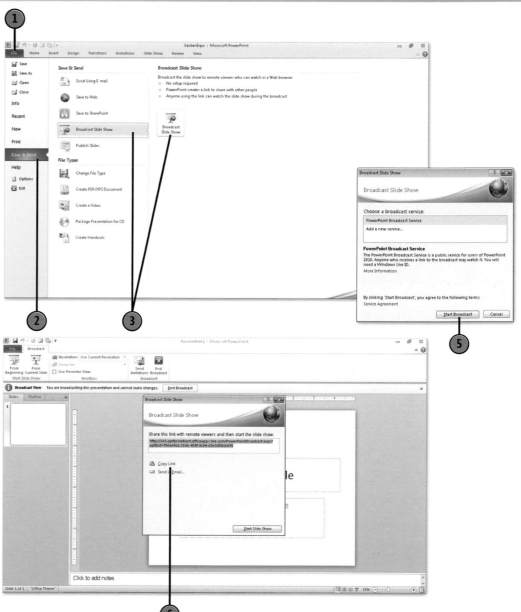

Run a Broadcast

① Follow the steps in the preceding task to set up the show and invite attendees. Then, click the Start Slide Show button in the Broadcast Slide Show dialog box to begin the online presentation.

② The slide show runs. Use the tools in the bottom-left corner to navigate through it:

- The left arrow moves back one slide.

- The right arrow moves forward one slide.

- Click the Options button, and use the Go To Slide command to move to a specific slide.

③ Press Esc, and then click the End Broadcast button that appears under the ribbon in the PowerPoint window to end the presentation.

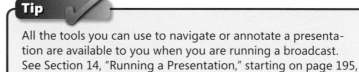

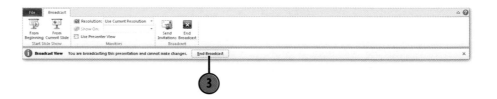

Tip

All the tools you can use to navigate or annotate a presentation are available to you when you are running a broadcast. See Section 14, "Running a Presentation," starting on page 195, for more about using these tools.

Creating a Video

You can save your PowerPoint presentation as a video that includes all the narration, timings, and animations you've built into it. People can then watch the video on their computing devices or you might post it on the Web on a video-sharing site such as YouTube.

① Click the File tab.

② Click Save & Send.

③ Click Create A Video.

④ Click the first drop-down list, and select the type of display you want to use for the video presentation: Computer & HD Displays, Internet And DVD, or Portable Devices.

⑤ Click the next list, and choose whether to use recorded timings and narrations with your video.

⑥ Use the spinner arrows beside Seconds To Spend On Each Slide to set the time each slide should be displayed in the video.

⑦ Click Create Video.

⑧ In the Save As dialog box, enter another name in the File Name box if you want to, and click Save. The video is saved to your SkyDrive folder. Go to the folder to view it.

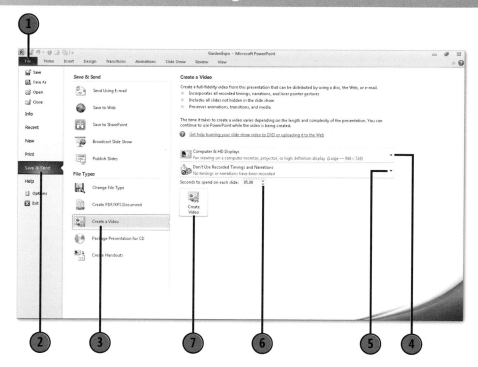

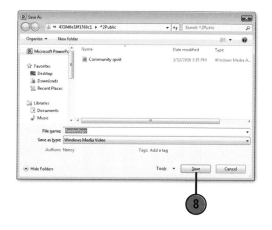

Tip ✓

When you play a video file, if you haven't used preset timings, you can use the backward and forward arrows to move from slide to slide.

Tip ✓

Saving a file as a video presentation can take a bit of time. Also, if you close PowerPoint before the video has been created, PowerPoint displays warning messages. It's a good idea to create a video when you have an errand to run or feel like multitasking with some other project.

Introducing Advanced PowerPoint Topics

The preceding sections of this book cover the topics you need to create most presentations and to use Microsoft PowerPoint 2010 efficiently. However, the advanced features that you can explore in this section help you work more efficiently.

You can develop a presentation that forms the basis of other presentations and save that presentation as a template. This step can save you a great deal of work setting up themes, layouts, and slide master settings for each new presentation.

Custom shows are subsets of the slides in a presentation that can be saved right inside the same file. Custom shows might contain only some of the slides in the presentation or rearrange the order of slides. For example, if you have a master presentation on your entire product line, you can save custom shows that focus on each product line separately and then show only the presentation that relates to an individual customer's needs.

A feature called Document Inspector allows you to search your files for hidden data and remove it before saving the file. Finally, you can add a digital signature to your presentation. A digital signature assures whoever opens the file that it comes from you.

Finally, once you're comfortable with the ribbon interface, you can explore customizing it to contain the tools you use most often.

Saving Your Own PowerPoint Templates

You can save any file in a template format (.potx). A template can contain various custom settings, such as changes you make to the slide master, custom layouts or animations you created, or themes and font choices you applied. Your templates can also contain text or graphic elements in placeholders. By using a template as the basis of a new presentation, you not only save time but guarantee a consistency of look and feel among all your presentations.

Save a Presentation as a Template

1 Make any settings or changes you want to the presentation, and then click the File tab.

2 Click Save As.

3 In the Save As Type list, choose PowerPoint Template.

4 Enter a name in the File Name box.

5 Click Save.

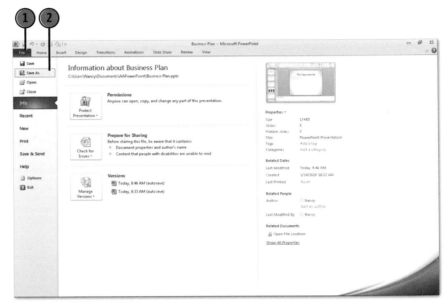

Tip ✓

Keep in mind that after you open a template, you need to save it as a regular PowerPoint presentation with a new name so that you don't overwrite the template with presentation-specific changes. For more information about saving files, see "Saving and Closing a PowerPoint Presentation" on page 49.

Tip ✓

If you have access to a Microsoft SharePoint site or a company intranet, you might consider sharing templates across an organization so that all presentations have a consistent company look and feel.

Tip ✓

If you or somebody else wants to use the template with an earlier version of PowerPoint, you should choose PowerPoint 97-2003 Template in step 3. This is useful if you are sharing a template with people working on earlier versions of the software.

Creating Custom Shows

The ability to create and store custom shows within a single presentation file offers you great flexibility. You can create several custom shows from one presentation by simply choosing the slides to include and reorganizing them in any way you want. The slides in a custom show remain identical to the corresponding slides in your main presentation, but by selecting and rearranging their order, you can create quite different shows to meet your viewers' needs.

Create a Custom Show

① Click the Slide Show tab.

② Click Custom Slide Show.

③ Click Custom Shows.

④ Click New in the Custom Shows dialog box.

⑤ Click a slide in the Slides In Presentation list.

⑥ Click Add. Repeat steps 5 and 6 to add all the slides you want in your custom show.

⑦ Click a slide in the Slides In Custom Show list.

⑧ Use the Move Up and Move Down buttons to reorganize the slide order. Repeat this step with other slides until your slides are in the order you want.

⑨ Enter a name in the Slide Show Name box.

⑩ Click OK.

⑪ Click Close to close the Custom Shows dialog box.

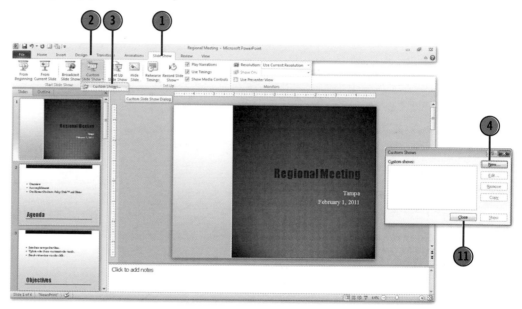

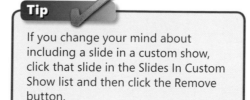

Tip

If you change your mind about including a slide in a custom show, click that slide in the Slides In Custom Show list and then click the Remove button.

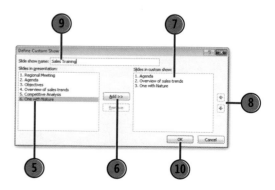

Try This!

If you created a custom show and need to edit it, click the Custom Slide Show button on the Slide Show tab. Select the show, and then click the Edit button. Use the preceding steps to add, remove, or rearrange the slides in the show, and then click OK.

Run a Custom Show

① Click the Slide Show tab.

② Click Custom Slide Show.

③ Click the name of the custom show. The show begins to run.

④ Use the navigation tools to move through the presentation. Press Esc to stop the show at any time.

Tip

You can use the Set Up Show dialog box (click the Set Up Slide Show button on the Slide Show tab) to set up your file to play a custom show whenever you click the Slide Show button. Just select the custom show you want to use from the Custom Show list.

See Also

For more information about using navigation tools in Slide Show view, see "Navigating Through Slides" on page 199.

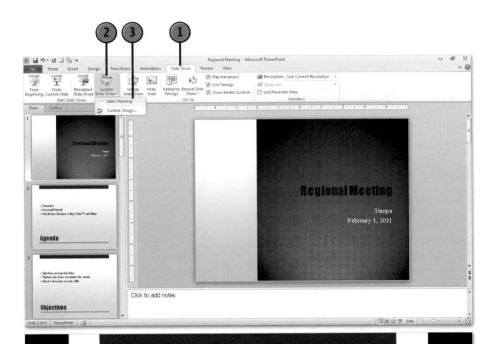

Removing Hidden Data with Document Inspector

When you intend to share a presentation, either by publishing it online or by handing it to somebody on a CD, it's a good idea to make sure there isn't any hidden data included. For example, a file might contain personal information about the author or document properties (called metadata) that you'd rather not share. You can use the Document Inspector feature in PowerPoint to remove such information.

Remove Hidden Data with Document Inspector

① Save a copy of your presentation with a new name.

② Click the File tab.

③ Click Info.

④ Click Check For Issues.

⑤ Click Inspect Document.

Tip

I start out this task by having you save a copy of the presentation because much of the data you delete using Document Inspector cannot be restored. If you don't save the file first, a window appears alerting you to this issue. The data that Document Inspector removes might be useful information for a presentation you are still working on, such as the date you last made a change to the presentation or invisible contents on slides. Working on a copy preserves that data in the original.

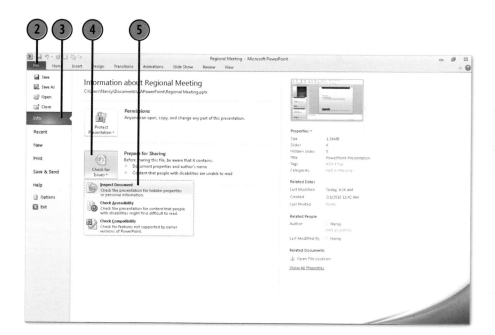

6 Select the various check boxes to choose what content to check for.

7 Click Inspect.

8 Click the Remove All buttons that appear in the results window.

9 Click Close to save the file with the selected data omitted.

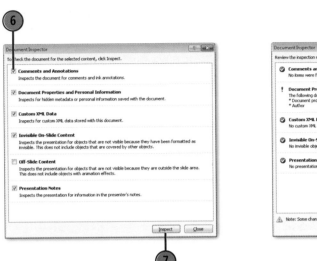

Try This!

If you want to manually edit your presentation properties to remove personal information instead of letting Document Inspector do all the work, click the File tab, choose Info, and then click the Properties button and choose Show Document Panel. Just delete any data in any field that you don't want included with the file.

Adding a Digital Signature

A digital signature is much like a handwritten signature on a check or other legal document. It can be used to ensure that the document was created by a particular person. In a world where computer files can contain potentially harmful materials, a digital signature helps to reassure recipients that a file was created by somebody they know and trust. You can use a digital signature provided by a third party that others can use to verify your document. You can also create one that serves only for you to verify that a document you open on your computer is your own.

Purchase a Third-Party Digital Signature Product

1. Be sure your computer is connected to the Internet, and then click the File tab.

2. Click Info, and then click Protect Presentation.

3. Click Add A Digital Signature.

4. In the confirming dialog box that appears, click Signature Services From The Office Marketplace.

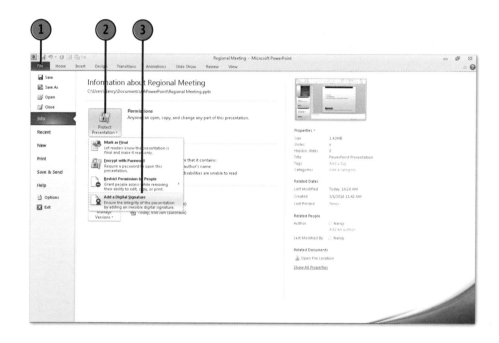

⑤ Select a digital signing provider in the list (which might change from time to time).

⑥ Click the Learn More link on the screen that appears and follow the steps to purchase a digital signature product or download a free trial. These steps might vary slightly from service to service.

Tip

Digital signing software can cost anywhere from under $100 to over $250. You might make this investment if it's important that you be sure that documents come from the person they purport to be from and that the contents of the document haven't been changed since they were signed.

Try This!

You can also use the Information Rights Management Service to authenticate the sender and recipient of files sent by e-mail to ensure that your files don't fall into the wrong hands. Click the File tab, and choose Info. Then click the Protect Presentation button, choose Restrict Permission By People, and choose Restricted Access. Follow the instructions to sign up for this service from Microsoft.

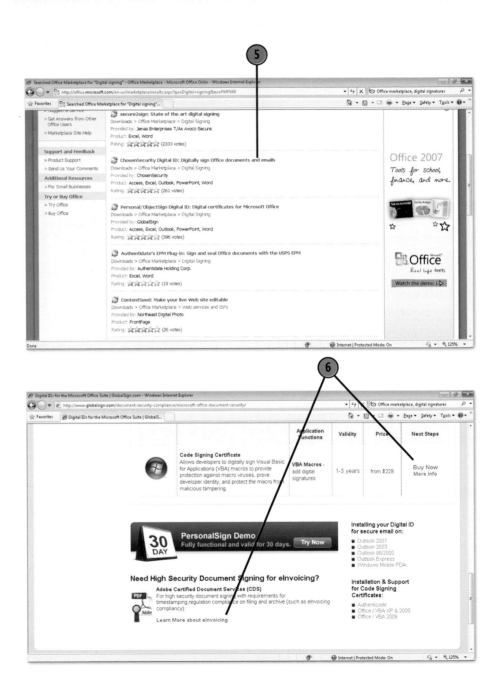

Create Your Own Digital Signature

(1) Save your file as a PowerPoint presentation, and then click the File tab.

(2) Click Info, and then click Protect Presentation.

(3) Click Add A Digital Signature.

(4) In the confirming dialog box, click OK. If you saved a digital signature before, skip to step 9.

(5) Click Create Your Own Digital ID.

(6) Click OK.

(7) Enter your name, e-mail address, organization, and location in the Create A Digital ID dialog box.

(8) Click Create.

(9) In the Sign dialog box, fill in the Purpose For Signing This Document box.

(10) Click Sign.

(11) In the Signature Confirmation dialog box, click OK.

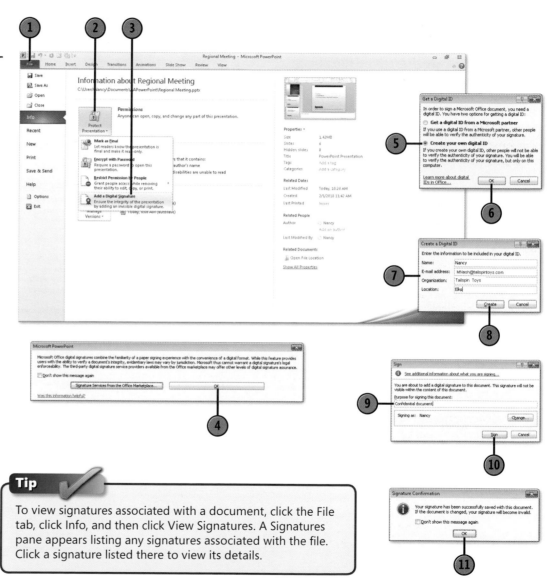

Tip

To view signatures associated with a document, click the File tab, click Info, and then click View Signatures. A Signatures pane appears listing any signatures associated with the file. Click a signature listed there to view its details.

Customizing the Ribbon

The idea behind the interface that started in Microsoft Office 2007 is that the most commonly used tools are present on the ribbon rather than buried in dialog boxes, and the tools you use less often, although accessible, aren't part of the main interface by default. Sometimes, the only way to access a function you might have used in a previous version of PowerPoint is to place a command on the ribbon.

Add Buttons to the Ribbon

(1) Choose Options from the File menu.

(2) Click Customize Ribbon.

(3) Click the arrow on the Choose Commands From list, and select a category of tool, or simply scroll down and choose the Commands Not In The Ribbon category.

(4) Click Main Tabs in the list on the right side, and click New Tab or New Group. Use the Rename button to rename the tab or group.

(5) Click a command in the list on the left, and then click the Add button to add it to the ribbon. Repeat this step for all the tools you want to add.

(6) Click OK.

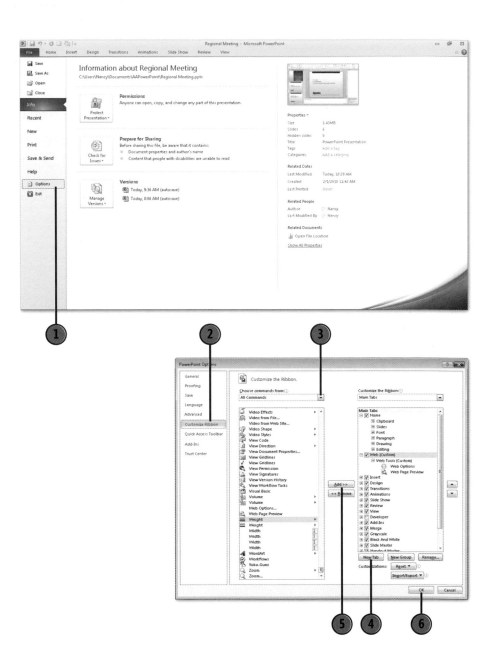

The new tab and tools are added to the ribbon.

Caution

Although you can add many tools to the ribbon, don't overdo it. Only add the tools you use most often, or add a tool to use a particular function, and then remove it to clear clutter off the ribbon.

Tip

If you change the ribbon and then want to put it back the way it was when you installed PowerPoint, go to the PowerPoint Options dialog box, select Customize Ribbon, and click Reset. The default ribbon settings are restored.

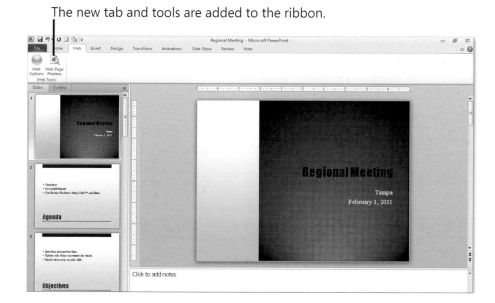

Remove or Rearrange Tools

① Choose Options from the File menu.

② Click Customize Ribbon.

③ Click an item in the list on the right.

④ Click Remove to remove it from the ribbon.

⑤ Click Move Up or Move Down to rearrange the tools.

⑥ Click OK to save your settings.

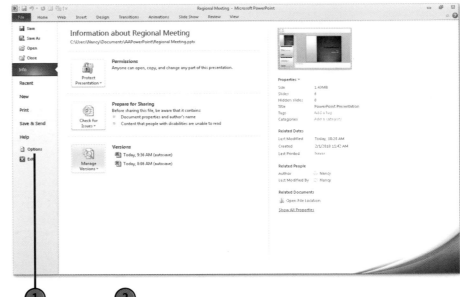

Tip

Be cautious about making changes to the ribbon because it might confuse others who use your copy of PowerPoint or even confuse you because the items on the ribbon will no longer match those in the Help system or books such as this one you use to learn PowerPoint.

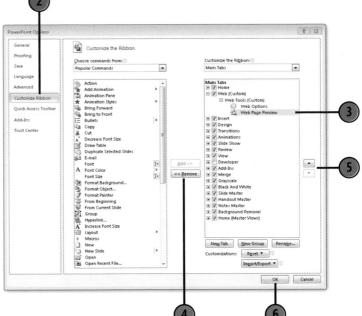

Index

Number

3-D effect, 80

A

action buttons, 139, 140
Action Settings dialog box, 140
Add-Ins tab in ribbon, 7, 24
Adobe Reader, 217
  obtaining copy, 222
advancing slides, 172
alignment of text
  in table cells, 117
  placeholder contents, 79
All Slide dialog box, 200
animation indicator in Slide Sorter view, 46
Animation Painter, 167, 176
  copying with, 16
animations, 167
  applying custom to object, 173
  modifying settings, 174
  preview, 177
  removing from object, 174
  reordering effects, 175
  running slide show without, 187
Animations tab in ribbon, 16
  Add Animation, 173
  Animation Pane, 174
  Preview, 177

annotations, 187, 202–205
  deleting, 205
  erasing, 204
  making on slides, 203
  pen style and color, 202
  saving, 48, 205
arrows, drawing, 139–140
Artistic Effects button, 160
Artistic Effects gallery, 11–12
audience handouts. *See* handouts
audio
  action button for playing, 140
  adding to transition, 170
  inserting, 135–136
  speed of transition and, 171
automatic slide advancement, 189
Available Templates And Themes list
  My Templates selection, 40

B

background, 165–166
  for handouts, 64
  gallery, 66
Backstage view, File tab, Print Options, 98
black screen, displaying temporarily, 198
blank presentation, opening, 38
bold text, 148
border line, 80
borders of tables, 116
brightness adjustment in picture, 160
Bring Forward button, 159
broadcasting slide shows, 18–19, 223–224

Broadcast Slide Show dialog box, 19, 223, 224
Browse For Themes command, 110
bulleted lists, alignment, 79
bullet points, 70
  in outlines, 82, 85
  placeholder for, 69
  timed sequence for appearance, 167
buttons, adding to Quick Access Toolbar, 89

C

callouts, drawing, 139–140
CDs, saving presentation to, 193
cells in tables
  aligning text, 117
  merging, 118
centered text, 79
Change Chart Type dialog box, 120
Character Spacing button, 148
Chart Layouts gallery, 121
charts, 119–123
  changing style and layout, 121–122
  inserting, 119–120
  legend display, 123
  types, 120, 121
Chart Styles gallery, 121
Choose A SmartArt Graphic dialog box, 15, 35, 130
Choose Commands From list, for Quick Access Toolbar, 30
Choose Theme Or Themed Document dialog box, 110

Esc key
    to end slide show, 198
Excel, 119
expanding outlines, 86

F

file format, for saving presentation, 49
file-management commands, 21
File menu, 6, 21, 23. *See also* Options
        command
    Close, 50
    displaying, 10
    Exit, 50
    New, 38, 39, 89
    Open, 41
    Print, 210, 212, 214
    Save, 49
    Save As, 49
    Save & Send, 222
filenames, for presentations, 49
File tab in ribbon, 21, 23
    Info
        Check For Issues, 231
        Permissions, 233
        Protect Presentation, 235
    New, 110
    Save & Send, 18, 185, 193
        Broadcast Slide Show, 223
        Create A Video, 225
        Save To Web, 218
fill color, 80, 149–150
finding
    clip art, 124
    existing presentations, 41
    text, and replacing, 76
    themes online, 110

Find Whole Words Only option, 76
first slide, moving to, 200
Fit Slide To Current Window button, 44
flipping objects, 156
floating toolbar, Mini toolbar as, 27
folders, opening, 39
Font dialog box, 144
    Character Spacing tab, 148
fonts, 104
    applying, 144
    for notes, 66
    symbols in, 71
    for themes, 112
    viewing list, 33
font schemes, 111
Fonts gallery, Create New Theme Fonts,
        112
footers
    adding date or time to, 209
    adding in Slide Master view, 56
    inserting, 208–209
    restoring placeholder after deleting, 56
    text for, 209
Format Legend dialog box, 123
Format Painter, 176
Format Shape dialog box, 153
    for text box, 141
Format tab in ribbon, 11, 32, 78
    Crop, 154
    Size group, 154
formatting
    for chart legend, 123
    for outlines, 88
    placeholders, 80
    text box, 141
formatting objects, 149–153
    fill color or effect, 149–150
    shape outline changes, 151

formatting text, 145–148
    color, 145–146
    Mini toolbar for, 27–28
    size changes, 147
frames for slides, 215
full-screen mode for running
        presentation, 47

G

galleries, 5, 11, 21, 22, 32–33
    Animation, 173
    Artistic Effects, 11–12
    Chart Layouts, 121
    Chart Styles, 121
    Corrections, 11–12
    Layout, 68, 104, 105
    Office Theme, 69
    Shape Fill, 150
    Shapes, 8
    Themes, 34, 104, 108
    Transitions, 168
    Video Styles, 162
    WordArt Styles, 32
gradient, 150
graphics, 82, 104, 113
    galleries of, 21, 22
    master, 57
    omitting master from individual slide,
        59
    removing background from handouts,
        64
gridlines, 156
grouping objects, 157–158
groups, 22

X

XPS file format, 222
  for sending slide show, 185

Y

YouTube, 225

Z

zoom slider, 93
  in Print Preview, 210
  in Slide Sorter view, 46
  in Slide Master view, 55
  for slide preview, 44, 82
Zoom To Page
  in Print Preview, 211

About the Author

Nancy Muir runs the Web site TechSmartSenior.com, where she offers advice on computing and the Internet to those over 50, and writes a column on computers and the Internet on Retirenet.com. She is also the author of more than 50 books on technology topics, including *Microsoft® Office PowerPoint® 2007 Plain & Simple* and the bestselling *Computers For Seniors For Dummies* from Wiley Publishing. Over the years, Nancy has worked in the software and book publishing industries as well as academia, and has served as a consultant to major technology companies.